D0253884

ELIJAH: ANOINTED AND STRESSED

The *Character and Charisma* series introduces us to people in the Bible and shows how their lives have much to teach us today. All the authors in the series use their communication skills to lead us through the biblical record and apply its encouragements and challenges to our lives today. Every volume contains an *Index of Life Issues* to enhance its usefulness in reference and application.

CHARACTER AND CHARISMA SERIES

Elijah

Anointed and Stressed

JEFF LUCAS

KINGSWAY PUBLICATIONS
EASTBOURNE

ISBN 0 85476 335 X

Produced by Bookprint Creative Services
P.O. Box 827, BN21 3YJ, England, for
KINGSWAY PUBLICATIONS LTD
Lottbridge Drove, Eastbourne, E Sussex BN23 6NT.
Printed in Great Britain.

*To my parents
who have smiled through the silence.
And to the Edwardsons:
Chris, Jeanne, Julia and Shayla.*

Contents

Acknowledgements

Friends are what make us rich. I am grateful that Kay and I have so many friends who want to live their lives out for the greatest cause ever known: the kingdom of God. I list the following names, not just because they 'deserve a mention', but because it is the lives of others, rather than words well written, that most powerfully influence and impact us. The drama of radical Christianity has been faithfully portrayed in the lives of my friends.

I am glad to be part of the Pioneer Team; to be among men and women of many years' experience, hardships, laughter and tears, who still refuse to take their eyes off Jesus. People like Adrian and Pauline Hawkes, who could have given up a hundred times, but remain faithful to God. Gerald Coates, both from a distance and now as a friend, has challenged, provoked and inspired me consistently. To raise one's voice above the background noise of bland religiosity is costly; I'm grateful, Gerald and Anona.

Locally, there are people like Malc and Kathy Garda, Mike and Katey Morris, Roger and Margaret Ellis and David and Sandra Cottrell, to name but a few. And in America, all those who serve on the Lifelight Board, as well as dear friends like Garry and Ruth Siegenthaler, Boyd and Sally Powers, Greg and Roxanne Hickman and the 'probable' Edwardsons . . . the list could go on!

7

All of these have seen something of what Elijah saw: the radical God.

And finally, to the people who quietly sacrifice the most when it comes to me: Kay, Kelly and Richard. You're the best!

Introduction

A Man Just Like Us. . .

With a sudden 'plop', the envelope landed on the door mat.

Are you like me when it comes to letters? I love the delicious sound of mail being thrust through the letterbox; it's a welcome noise, one guaranteed to motivate me to forsake the warmth of my bed, and rush quickly downstairs to gather up the daily prize. But, as I picked up the envelope and examined it for some clue as to its contents (which is much more fun than just ripping the thing open, though slightly less logical), my heart sank. Printed in lurid red letters the words '*Victory Report!!!*' screamed at me. This was a familiar and unwelcome letter.

It arrived with monthly monotony—a news-sheet from a nationally-known evangelist. The epistle had a threefold purpose. It provided points for prayer, showed photographs of the man himself (preaching, laughing, crying, walking his dog and smiling at his wife and occasionally walking his wife and smiling at his dog) and then it told me how to send money and exactly why I should send it, immediately, *now*!

None of these things particularly troubled me: the man had integrity and a powerful ministry, and even the high-pressured sales technique no longer bothered me. I simply accepted it as part of the American culture.

9

What seriously jarred me was the fact that every report, month after month, was a *victory* report. Victory, victory, all the way. . . .

As I stood there, the unthinkable came to mind. I thought how very welcome it would be to receive an envelope headed 'Defeat Report'. Not as exciting or sensational, but certainly a little more reflective of reality. How wonderful it would be to receive a defeat report, just once. . . .

Now I'm not a defeatist. I'm uneasy in the company of those dour-faced negative Evangelicals who vote against joy, noise, fun or, for that matter, victory, while maintaining a facial expression that communicates pure, sacred constipation. Words like 'warfare' and 'victory' are often on my lips. I don't consider triumph to be a post-death experience.

No, my problem is more with the unreality of the monthly 'bliss bulletin'; the idea that some Christians (particularly the famous types) breeze through life in a constant state of blessed ecstasy for twenty-six hours of the day, and that everything they touch, spiritually speaking, turns to gold or, in this case victory.

The truth is that good Christians, even great Christians, experience times when life is painful, boring, confusing and sometimes downright tragic. General William Booth, founder of the Salvation Army, came to the place of total defeat more than once. His heavy itinerant ministry, with the accompanying loneliness that extensive travelling brings, caused him to write the following to his wife Catherine: 'I wonder whether I could not get something to do in London of some kind, some secretaryship or something respectable that would keep us going. I know how difficult things are to obtain without friends or influence, as I am fixed. But we must hope against hope, I suppose.'*

To know that even the great General went through these feelings is quite encouraging. Perhaps that's why the Bible is so honest, providing us with stark portraits of real, flesh-and-blood human beings who laughed and cried, believed and doubted, walked in holiness and smeared their lives with immorality. Scripture never presents us with a casebook of grinning, larger-than-life heroes. Even the most prominent are shown without theatrical makeup. Samson, anointed mighty warrior, who could overthrow hordes of Philistines, but was conquered by the lethal combination of his own ego and hormones. Peter, key spokesman in the early church, whose shadow brought instantaneous healing—and the one who had walked around with his mouth in fifth gear and his brain in neutral, until finally the sound of the cock crowing silenced his boasting.

The Bible never whitewashes failure—or defeat. Paul the apostle was one of those stressed-out saints, and he did rather well as a believer. Much of the New Testament flowed from his pen. Abundant miracles filled his life. He took day trips to heaven, 'caught up in the Spirit' as he put it, but, because he never lost touch with reality, he still knew how to draft a defeat report. Writing to the contentious Corinthians, he bares his heart: 'We do not want you to be uninformed, brothers, about the hardships we suffered in the province of Asia. We were under great pressure, far beyond our ability to endure, so that we despaired even of life. Indeed, in our hearts we felt the sentence of death' (2 Cor 1:8–9).

Talk about straight shooting! Imagine receiving a

---

* Begbie, *The Life of General William Booth*, p 422.

newsletter like that today. 'Greetings, beloved prayer partners and financial supporters. We want you to know the truth. We're fed up. Life has been a pain this month. We can't take much more of this. In fact, we're just a bit suicidal. Yours sincerely. . . .'

Jeremiah was another serious realist who often experienced wildly fluctuating emotions. Jeremiah 20:13 reveals a prophet on an emotional roller-coaster: 'Sing to the Lord! Give praise to the Lord! He rescues the life of the needy from the hands of the wicked.' That's the positive bit. Well done, Jeremiah—but now hear the very next verses:

> Cursed be the day I was born! May the day my mother bore me not be blessed! Cursed be the man who brought my father the news, who made him very glad, saying, 'A child is born to you—a son!' May that man be like the towns the Lord overthrew without pity. May he hear wailing in the morning, a battle cry at noon. For he did not kill me in the womb, with my mother as my grave, her womb enlarged for ever. Why did I ever come out of the womb to see trouble and sorrow and to end my days in shame? (Jer 20:14–18).

Apparently, Jeremiah was the type who kicked the dog when he felt low, and then also kicked his mother and the local newspaper editor (the man who announced his birth) as well!

And so we come to Elijah. What a mighty man he was! His name means 'Yahweh—he is the real God'. Every time Elijah introduced himself, he made a powerful statement about the convictions that burned in his heart. When we come to consider the stressed-out Elijah, we do well to remember that we are discussing a seasoned veteran of faith, not an unstable novice.

This is the man who spoke to death, and death died, as

he raised up the widow's son. Before we write off Elijah as some weakling, let us check our diary. When was the last time we saw life surge into a corpse because of our prayers? This was the man who spoke to the clouds and instructed them to hold back the rain—and they obeyed! Fire fell from heaven at his command.

It was Elijah who stood fearlessly before the highest authority in the land, together with her moody, wimp of a husband, and pointed the prophetic finger accusingly at the evil pair—'You are the cause of all the trouble in Israel!' (see 1 Kings 18:17–18).

Just in case you're still not convinced about the spiritual magnitude of the man, remember that it was Elijah who challenged 450 Baal prophets to the Old Testament equivalent of the gunfight at the OK Corral—and he won!

However, it was this same hero who, despite his calling and his undeniable anointing, became so stressed out that he wanted to die. No major sin had been committed. Far from being backslidden, he had experienced more of the raw power of God than most of us will ever see.

He was, however, called, anointed and stressed out. That's why I want you to come with me and look at the glorious ministry of Elijah which climaxed at Carmel, and from there, come to a lonely cave pitted into the hillside of Mount Sinai. Although I have used a dramatic approach to Elijah's story, I have tried as far as is possible to base the story on solid biblical, historical and archaeological facts.

Our journey will not take us through intricate principles of stress management, helpful though many of those truths are. Neither will this be a '470 ways beginning with Z to get rid of all stress by next Wednesday' type of book.

My aim is twofold. I want you to see some reality, because reality is liberating. It's so refreshing to know that you're not the only one who walks through dark days.

I discovered that simple principle when addressing a leadership forum recently. We were discussing 'post-preaching syndrome', and I happened to mention that some of my greatest struggles of faith have hit me while driving home from successful meetings. People have been saved and encouraged, God has clearly moved—and then I'm heading home down the motorway late at night, and suddenly the thought surfaces: 'I wonder if there really is a God?'

The leaders let out a gasp. For some it was an expression of shock that I should have used that dirty word 'doubt' so openly, but for most it was an exclamation of relief; a moment to say, 'Thank God I'm not alone in my struggles.' Reality, like all truth, will set us free.

My other aim is to point you towards a God who doesn't always choose to answer all of our questions, but who is big enough to help us through the days of defeat. Elijah wasn't sent packing by God. Rather, as we will see, he was gently recharged and recommissioned, and returned to blessing and usefulness.

It was David who testified that God 'restored his soul'. The phrase is enlightening, because 'restore' is a shepherding word, and David, because of his working background, used it advisedly. Apparently, sheep occasionally go to sleep in hollows, and the result is that they end up rolling over on their backs, becoming totally and helplessly immobile. Unless someone helps them, they will quickly drown in their own lung fluids. Struggling and kicking, they wait for help—or death. Hopefully, the shepherd will come and restore them—a gentle but firm nudge that will roll them back over.

Perhaps you're going through a time right now when, like Elijah, you've had enough. You're spiritually alive, but kicking. Not with vibrancy and life, but with frustration and despair.

I pray that as we share a cave with Elijah for a while, you will meet a God who can nudge us out into light and life again—and that you will discover that the God of Elijah is your God too.

Jeff Lucas

1

Early Days

Sweat glossed the woman's contorted face, a mask of pain, eyes sunken hollows in the candlelight, a low moan now with each new contraction. She was spent, not an ounce of energy left, but the midwife who fussed around her bed urged her on: one last terrible push. In the flickering shadows sat two other women, family friends, muttering their commentaries, experts in their own eyes at least. Minutes earlier the humble bedchamber had reverberated with the woman's screams, her frantic begging for it all to be over. But now she was too tired even to cry out—she had to be delivered of this baby now. Another few minutes and she would surely die.

Outside the house sat her husband; nervous, waiting. He had steeled himself during the screaming; the sudden quiet alarmed him more. He couldn't go in of course; it was unheard of, unthinkable. So he waited alone. How they wanted this baby now! When they had first discovered the pregnancy, there had been an immediate sense of panic, for this meant one more mouth to feed, and times were hard for the likes of them. Israel was experiencing something of a booming economy—for the rich. The wealthy landowners seemed possessed of a demonic greed, demanding more and more rent from the tenant farmers until there was just nothing left to fill empty bellies. How would they manage?

However, as the months had gone by and the child had enlarged in the womb, so grew a strange sense of peace in their hearts. They were both loyal followers of the true God. Not for them the dark foolishness of the Baals. Whatever the royal family was up to—whatever the rich folk worshipped—they would stay true to Yahweh. And as they prayed, so there came a sense that somehow, in a way they couldn't begin to explain, Yahweh himself was involved in the birth of this child. The thought was staggering, and perhaps would appear to some as pretentious for such ordinary folk to consider, but they had held it in their hearts, comfort for the future. As the man sat and pondered the silence that had fallen on the house, he prayed out loud: 'Lord of hosts! Give me a son.'

Suddenly the silence was shattered. Not this time by another scream, but by laughter and excited chatter. The child was here! Without waiting to be asked, casting propriety to the wind, he rushed inside, and was immediately shocked to see the condition of his wife; her hair lank, her thighs bloodied, perhaps death was on her. And then she managed the faintest of smiles: all was well.

The child was put to the breast, and suddenly fresh energy seemed to surge into the woman. The midwife spoke: 'Give praise to your God . . . he's given you a son.'

The man smiled broadly, and ran his palm gently over his wife's fevered forehead, pushing back a hair that had strayed into the corner of her eye. It was time to name this boy, this son of his. They had talked and laughed and prayed about it a dozen times these last few months, and they both knew the answer. If God gave them a boy, then the lad would be known by a name that would publicly honour the true God. Such an act was dangerous. It was like thumbing a nose at the palace; a slap in the face of the so-called gods. But the name had been chosen, and they would not go back on their decision.

The name had a meaning: 'The Lord, he is the real God.'

Eli-yah.

Elijah.

Setting the scene: the home

Gilead was a place of striking, rugged scenery; beautiful to share, terrifyingly quiet for the lonely traveller. The Jordan River separated Gilead from the rest of Israel, both geographically and culturally. Thick, shaggy forests covered the hillsides—lush land where large herds of sheep grazed, and mountain streams skipped and trickled lazily down. Towering cliffs began in limestone and were peaked in black volcanic rock. The prophets sang about its picturesque views; the sick clamoured for its famous spice, the balm of Gilead, which was reputed to ease pain.

The locals were like their land: separate and proud. They looked with disdain at those who farmed beyond the Jordan, sneered at them as compromisers, lovers of the Baals. Many of them lived and worked in the open air; tough, serious shepherds. Their black Bedouin goathair tents were clumped together in makeshift villages, enabling them to live in the heights during summer and move to the valleys in wintertime. Dressed in camel-hair cloaks held together by thick, crude leather belts, they made a stark contrast to the sophistication of the city-dwellers, and the affluent finery of those privileged enough to be part of the Royal Samarian Court.

Even their speech set them apart. They spoke with such a strong accent that in times of war they distinguished friend from foe simply by asking them to say one word: 'Shibboleth'(Judg 12:5–6). The uninitiated enemy, unable to imitate the dialect, was found out within seconds.

Elijah was born 2,900 years ago in Gilead, in the little town of Tishbe. It was not an auspicious place for a great man to begin his life. Tishbe was so obscure that archaeologists can't even tell us its exact location.

Setting the scene: the nation

For many years Israel had been rotting in serious moral and spiritual decay, and by the time Elijah had reached adulthood, they had come to an all-time low—the bottom of the pit. The golden age of David and Solomon was finished. Six kings had come and gone in just fifty-eight years—a royal rogues' gallery if ever there was one. The first two of these were idolaters, the third was a murderer, the fourth was an alcoholic *and* a murderer, the fifth was accused of 'spiritual treason' and the sixth was described as worse than the previous five before him.

Now the seventh king was on the throne, and incredibly he beat even number six—an expert in evil. He was Ahab, and his wife was the infamous Jezebel.

It is unlikely that the royal marriage was truly happy, because it was the fruit of shrewd politics rather than real love. Ahab and Jezebel came together as a result of a peace treaty struck by Ahab's father, Omri, with the Phoenicians in the north. Omri was a brilliant tactician. He came to power after four years of raging civil war in Israel, when the army and the ruling classes had been at loggerheads. Omri had held the loyalty of the military. Tibni, son of Ginath, had become the darling and hero of the ruling classes, but Omri had prevailed and become King.

Now it was time for strength and consolidation, and an alliance with the powerful Phoenicians seemed good for everyone. Both Israel and Phoenicia were under threat from the Syrians, so a co-operative treaty appeared to make a great deal of sense (terrible choices often appear logical). To seal the deal, young Prince Ahab was given in marriage to Princess Jezebel, daughter of Eshbaal, the Priest-King of Tyre, a massively powerful nation which even had colonies in faraway Europe. The marriage was totally forbidden by the law of God, but who was worried? Integrity is sacrificed daily on altars of convenience: the union of Ahab and Jezebel was 'a good deal' for both countries—or so it seemed. It is uncertain whether Jezebel wed Ahab as the already reigning King or when he was still Crown Prince. All we know for sure is that the marriage took place between 878 and 872 BC; Ahab ruled as King from 874–853 BC. And what is certain is that the rule of Ahab and Jezebel cast a deep, dark shadow over Israel; a twenty-one-year season of death.

When Jezebel moved house and home to Samaria to begin a new life, she brought her fascination with the occult with her. Jezebel was a devoted, perhaps fanatical, worshipper of Baal Melqart, the chief god of Tyre (the name Malqart means 'King of the City', a territorial principality). Baal worship was nothing new to Israel; they had long been worshipping Baals, but the arrival of the Princess Jezebel of Tyre marked the beginning of a new era of idolatry.

It was quite common for foreign queens to be allowed to practise their own religion. Solomon's wives had littered the western slopes of the Mount of Olives with their occultic shrines, but this had no real effect on the general population as theirs was a private indulgence. But Jezebel was different. She was almost evangelical in her occultic zeal. She had a huge temple erected in honour of Melqart, and then began to turn on those who insisted that Yahweh alone was God. She was a demonised mass-murderess who nursed a pathological hatred for anything to do with the real 'owner' of the area (and the universe with it), Yahweh, establishing a programme of wholesale execution for God's prophets. Fortunately, God had his mole in the palace: a high-ranking minister of state called Obadiah, who was in charge of the royal household. Obadiah was the original double agent. Risking certain death if discovered, he set up a rescue programme, hiding 100 of God's prophets away in caves. He kept them supplied with food and water as well (1 Kings 18:4).

By the time Ahab became King, Jezebel had built up a full-time staff of 450 Baal prophets, plus an extra team of 400 prophets of the goddess Asherah. She was a clever opportunist, the real source of power in the land.

Baal worship was far more than an alternative theory, an occult philosophy. It was an active, energetic pulse of evil which became hugely popular with the masses. It's not hard to see why Baalism was enjoying a revival, quite apart from the credibility that came with royal patronage. Baal worship played on the perverse human hunger for occult power and bizarre sex.

The idea that God—or the gods—can be bought or bribed has always been attractive to arrogant man. That is why some folk would far rather whip themselves, put needles into their bodies or drag themselves up a shrine hill on their knees, than accept God's scandalous offer of free forgiveness. Human pride loves to pay—it feeds our sense of self-sufficiency. Baal, therefore, was a hired hand-god: give the right offering, friend, and all will be well with you and yours. Your cosmic insurance premium will be paid up, and disaster won't come near you. Even if you have to cut yourself with knives in the process (as Baal prophets often did), it will be worth it all in the end, because you'll get your heart's desire.

Worshippers of Baal also believed that the gods (who were obviously somewhat slow on the uptake) needed humans to act out their prayerful instructions in order to get the message through. This was a society that heavily relied on agriculture, so a bumper harvest was a priority. Baal was supposed to have power over drought and sterility, so the dramatic prayer followed logically: 'Listen, Baal, we need you to help our seeds to be fertilised, and in case you're not sure what it is we're on about, here are a few dozen shrine prostitutes, male and female, acting out a fertility ritual just to make it absolutely clear.' The worshippers of Baal were driven on by the same frenzied spirit that feeds the effluent tide of pornography today.

The third and most hideous facet of the Baal cult was child sacrifice. Why would any mother allow her newborn child to be taken, warm from the breast, and then watch it be thrown into a blazing furnace? What kind of madness drives a member of the human race to do such a thing? Such behaviour may defy logical explanation, but the fact remains that it did happen—and still happens. Today's sacrifices have an air of clinical sophistication about them, but none the less, millions of unborn children are still executed in the names of more modern gods. Is the stinging saline injected by the abortionist so very different from the ancient fire built in Baal's honour? The methods may be different, but the result is the same—the naked slaughter of the innocent. Perhaps we have become hardened to the silent screams. Shed blood and violent death are no strangers to us now.

Likewise, Jezebel was no stranger to death: her own father had assumed rule in Tyre because he had taken on the role of political assassin. According to the historian Josephus, Jezebel's father had been a long-time priest of Astarte who had murdered his brother, King Phelles, ascending to the throne at the age of thirty-six. Her father's name gives an interesting insight to the whole-hearted commitment of this evil family to the occult: it simply means 'with Baal'. The atmosphere of her child-hood was an ideal environment to breed a psychopathic temperament. For as long as she could remember, human life had been cheap.

This then was the religion of Jezebel: arrogant, porno-graphic and running with the blood of the innocents. And she was no passive, mildly-interested royal—she was a religious maniac.

Ahab, however, was a completely different character from his wife. A moral weakling, he was a man who lacked conviction and decisiveness. He didn't even share his bride's single-minded commitment to the Baals. In fact, it would seem that Ahab was incapable of being single minded about anything. He was just willing to worship whomever and whatever, as long as it kept every-body happy. Ever the man to please, Ahab had himself set up a special sacred stone monument to the Baals near to the altar of the occultic temple and, just to be on the safe side, he threw in a pole in honour of goddess Asherah for good measure (1 Kings 16:33).

He even named three of his children in honour of Yah-weh—Jehoram ('Yahweh is high'), Ahaziah ('Yahweh has taken hold') and Athaliah ('Yahweh is exalted'). Ahab was a man of religious tokenism, willing to treat the God of heaven and the devil of hell like good luck charms, to use and discard at will. Sometimes his carelessness backfired. Years earlier, Joshua had put a curse on the city of Jericho, and had decreed that anyone who tried to rebuild would be smitten by the loss of their children. Scripture records that a man named Heil attempted to flout the warning and go ahead with a construction programme anyway, which he did 'in the time of Ahab'. That little phrase means that it was done with Ahab's knowledge, even perhaps decreed by Ahab, as Jericho was right on a major trade route. Never mind what the man of God had said in the past. Ahab didn't have to risk anything personally anyway. It was Heil's head—and the heads of his children—that was on the block, and it was he who ultimately suffered judgement.

In the Walt Disney cartoon film *Robin Hood*, the evil Prince John is portrayed as a skinny lion who shouts and screams and wields absolute power, but sticks his thumb in his mouth and goes into a tantrum whenever life gets difficult. Ahab was such a character—one of those moody types who would sulk like a child when he didn't get his own way. On one occasion he was desperate to gain control of a vineyard in Jezreel, but the owner, Naboth, wouldn't strike a deal. The great King's response? 'So Ahab went home, sullen and angry because Naboth the Jezreelite had said, "I will not give you the inheritance of my fathers." He lay on his bed sulking and refused to eat' (1 Kings 21:4).

His immaturity and lack of moral backbone are further illustrated by the way he allowed himself to be shamelessly manipulated by his wife. Scripture provides a most pathetic epitaph: 'There was never a man like Ahab, who sold himself to do evil in the eyes of the Lord, urged on by Jezebel his wife' (1 Kings 21:25).

When Naboth wouldn't co-operate, a simple 'frame-up' job was set in motion at the suggestion of his conniving Jezebel, and this resulted in the execution of the unfortunate businessman. Ahab, like a rich, spoiled brat who can only lust after other children's toys, was free to take possession of the vineyard.

So we have King Ahab and Queen Jezebel—enemies of God and his people—a manic pair, driven, unpredictable and ruthless, in tandem for Satan. As one writer puts it:

> By himself Ahab would have been a menace . . . plainly an opportunist, he seemed to have few convictions or scruples. But he was not by himself. Jezebel was by his side, using her prestige and influence as insidiously and maliciously as possible. The corruption of Canaanite religion had long been seeping in from the Israelite's Canaanite neighbours, but under Jezebel it was pumped from the palace with extraordinary pressure.*

A rude awakening

It had been one of those long, balmy days that often give birth to vivid childhood memories. The two teenage lads, more men than boys now really, had chased their way around a thousand rocks, dangled their feet luxuriously in the cool mountain streams, and now it was time for home: a good day. The sun was slipping quickly behind distant Carmel. Their bodies ached the pleasant ache of energy spent, fun enjoyed. Their stomachs were hungry for food, their limbs ready to melt into sleep.

---

* William Sanford LaSor, David Allen Hubbard, Frederic William Bush, *Old Testament Survey* (Grand Rapids, Michigan: William B. Erdmans Publishing Co, 1982), p 266.

Then, with just a mile to go, they heard the drums, and they immediately knew. This was what Father had warned them about repeatedly. He had commanded them in no uncertain terms to stay away from the evening feasts. But curiosity drew them like a magnet, away from Father's wise words. Their minds made up, they began to run towards the sound of the drums.

They were perfectly safe in the lengthening shadows of the rocks, yet later they both admitted to being frozen to the spot with terror. A fierce, angry fire tore with rage at the gathering dusk, and the figures of the Baal priests circled around it seemed contorted; caught more in spasm than in dance, as they stamped and screamed, round and round. Wide eyed, the boys watched as the dancers, apparently mesmerised by their magic and their music, began to stab themselves savagely with flint knives, the blood from pierced fingers and palms running over the knuckles and forearms as they waved their arms high.

And then the boys found themselves blushing to the very roots of their hair as members of the crowd began to peel off their clothing and join in with the writhing ritual. There was no subtlety or finesse in this orgy. The gyrating and thrusting was obvious even to unworldly teenage eyes. Men ran their hands greedily over the bodies of women they had never met; strangers now in a union spawned by Satan. Some preferred members of their own sex. The shadows held no attraction; discretion was irrelevant. In the harsh glare of the fire, many were already locked in a loveless celebration of lust as, like panting animals on heat, they clutched and clawed and pushed and yelled. . . .

It went on for a long time. The air was filled with obscene sounds of perverse desires fulfilled; human putrification. The boys just knelt there, unable to speak, and occasionally they pushed their faces hard onto the rock to block out the gross images that stained the night. And then, just when they thought it was all over, and that all the evil was spent, they saw the woman, just a young girl really, standing with a bundle of cloth in her arms. She was nervous, shifting her weight from one foot to the other, waiting. Conflicting shadows of emotion raced across her face: one moment an expression of spiritual intensity, as she tried to enter into the worship—and then, the passion would suddenly fade, wiped off and replaced by a look of bewilderment, a little lost child face. At last, as if to settle the matter, her moment came. The gyrating priests broke their tortured circle and allowed her to step in. The drums grew louder, and then suddenly, with one violent beat, everything stopped dead. The dancers seemed frozen to the spot; every one of them now gazing intently at the girl. And suddenly her eyes seemed like empty sockets. Tears stained her cheeks as very slowly she began to open the bundle of cloths.

Watching from the shadows, Elijah felt like his heart was going to stop beating. As the grubby cloths were unwrapped, he saw the pink, pure skin of a baby, not more than a month old.

As if to urge the woman on, the music began again, louder, manic now. From deep within the woman came a long moan, the sound of a soul in torture, as she flung her child, arms still outstretched for the comfort of a mother's embrace, into the roaring flames. Mercifully the music muffled the child's final cries, and the woman crumpled to the ground.

Elijah pounded the rock that sheltered him; tears mingled with anger and frustration. And for him, innocence died with the child. And lest we diffuse our own anger at the awfulness of this slaughter by consigning the event to history, let us remember the saline drip and the gaping, hungry tongs of our day. And as we remember and weep, we remind ourselves that the so-called 'ascent of man' is a myth.

2

Foundations

Perhaps it was out in the Gilead highlands that the young Elijah first became aware of the living God himself. The campfire stories at the end of the day had played their part in influencing his thinking, but out there alone, with only the trickling of the mountain streams breaking the hot, still silence, he would walk and think and consider life. What growing boy out in the hills has not called out his own name, and clapped his hands just to hear the echo reply? But there was another name now that Elijah would call out, enjoying the sound of it bouncing around hillsides: 'Yahweh!'

And one day, he sensed a reply that came, not echoing and booming around the hillsides, but from somewhere within himself. A voice seemed to be calling *his* name.

*   *   *

The passion had begun with prayer—most great things do. Rumours about the dark goings on at the palace had been hurriedly whispered behind cupped hands in the market place. But, as time went on, the picture became sickeningly clear—the disease had spread like an epidemic.

31

Israel was infested with Baal worship. Some had spoken out about the disgrace that was blighting the land. Perhaps the more earthy cracked unkind jokes about the beautiful Jezebel. She loved to paint her eyes with kohl, a mixture of burned frankincense and almond shells, primitive mascara. She was famous for her arched eyebrows and the jet black lines that edged her eyelids. But her name would have triggered a thousand private jokes. In her own language, 'Jezebel' means 'where is Baal?'. In Hebrew, 'Zebel' means 'refuse' or 'dung', the irony of which would surely not have been lost on the poor. 'She's powerful, she's pretty, but she's. . . .'

Eventually, however, even the whispers of dissent would have faded, hushed by the news that the Yahweh prophets were being arrested and executed. At a religious level, many of the people seemed blissfully unconcerned. After all, wasn't Yahweh just another one of the Baals anyway?

However, Elijah, now a grown man, couldn't surrender his heart and mind to that spiritual pragmatism; and what began within him as a flickering, tiny flame of anger and disgust at the apostasy of the people had been steadily fanned into a raging furnace of fury. The Spirit of God served as divine bellows, coaxing the flames, urging them to rise and roar. But with the fresh passion and indignation came a sense of helplessness: what could he, just another country boy, do about the situation? The answer was obvious, for it was the only answer—he could pray.

And how he prayed! The Epistle of James tells us that he prayed 'earnestly'—the exact translation is, 'He prayed in prayer.' This was no hurried notelet to God, scrawled in between more pressing and important engagements: 'Dear Lord, bless me, bless the family, bless Israel and sort out the brains of the royal family. Amen.' This was a prayer symphony of angry tears, whispers and shouts, strident walking up and down, up and down, and a body pressed hard into the earth, shoulders shaking, a fist hammering the ground; a repetitive, dull thud as he pounded out his demands to God.

Be warned—'praying in prayer' is dangerous! Only those who mean business should try it, because it inevitably leads to radical action. Intercession is a bridge between interest and involvement. Real praying can never say, 'God, would you please get involved with this situation, as I, your passive servant, don't want to bother.' Prayer is a springboard, a trigger that really should carry a government health warning: 'Prayer is risky, and may seriously affect your capacity for ease, comfort and general mediocrity.'

'Praying with prayer' is focused, strategic praying too. Elijah knew the Law of God; he had read and reread those old words, and he knew that they were still true:

> Love Yahweh your God and serve him with all your heart. If you do, he will send rain on your land when it is needed, in the autumn and in the spring, so that there will be corn, wine and olive oil for you, and grass for your cattle. You will have all the food that you want. Do not let yourselves be led away from Yahweh to serve other gods. If you do, Yahweh will become angry with you. *He will hold back the rain*, and your ground will become too dry for the crops to grow . . . (Deut 11:13–17).

One phrase gripped his heart and wouldn't let go. 'He will hold back the rain . . . he will hold back the rain . . . he will hold. . . .'

So, nervously at first, for it seemed such a terrible prayer, he began to ask for a divine drought. The more he prayed, the more logical the prayer seemed, for a drought would certainly be an attention grabber. The common belief of the new, evil religion was that Baal was the god of rain ('Rkb-rpt', 'the Rider in the Clouds'), and that Baal lived in a house in the sky which had a 'rain window' in it. An ancient inscription has been found that celebrates this Ugaritic myth:

> Let a window be opened in the house
> An aperture in the midst of the palace
> And let a cleft be opened in the cloud.

Another declared: 'Baal . . . makes his voice heard in the clouds, he shoots forth lightning, and sends the beneficent rain. . . .'

Since Baal was now supposed to be the one who provided rain, the absence of it in a drought was believed to be the sign of the death of Baal, overcome by the god Mot, the god of death.

In every way, drought would be a loud and clear message from Yahweh! And so the asking turned into pleading, and then the pleading stopped and he found himself almost commanding God to do just what he had promised to do in the book of the Law. But even if and when drought came, would Ahab and Jezebel recognise the judgement of Yahweh, or would they just double their efforts and increase their Baal bribes, perhaps even switching allegiance to Mot? There was only one solution: someone would have to go to the palace and tell them.

*　　*　　*

Perhaps it started as an idle daydream. One of those 'If I saw that King I'd jolly well give him a piece of my mind and some of God's mind too' type fantasies. We all take those familiar and fantastic mental journeys—ideas that we flirt with once in a while, and then send packing with an embarrassed smile.

This daydream, however, wouldn't go away. And it was always the same: he saw himself marching straight into the inner chambers of the royal palace. He'd square himself up, look the King straight in the eye, and proclaim the word of God in a calm, clear voice. A wild, crazy idea that refused to be vaporised by reality.

And slowly the truth dawned. God was broadcasting daydreams on Elijah's personal wavelength, quietly calling him to be the answer to his own prayers. The God of all Israel was looking for a divine messenger boy, with the palace of Samaria as first delivery point. Elijah took a deep breath and prepared himself for the toughest challenge of his life.

Take time out for a moment, and imagine what it could have been like. A few modern analogies may help us to understand.

A hardline Protestant marches alone down the Falls Road, Belfast; enemy country for him. His left hand holds high a Union Jack flag; a gaudy, defiant clenched fist. And now he lifts his voice with the colours: 'Down with the IRA! Justice for the killers! God save the Queen. . . .' Menacing eyes stare, wide with amazement at the foolish, suicidal mania of the man.

Or picture the single, mad Zionist who stands up in a crowd of Palestinians and loudly denounces the PLO in general and Yassa Arafat in particular.

Imagine 'blasphemous' author Salman Rushdie of *Satanic Verses* fame, alone and helpless in Iran, a huge price on his head and plenty of fundamentalist zealots ready and willing to claim it.

Think of the raw, stomach-clenching fear that would stiffen every muscle in your body as you realised that you were totally, utterly alone, and that every living soul was an enemy. That's probably how Elijah felt as he marched towards Samaria, the outline of the hilltop palace seeming both to summon and threaten him. A slow, agonising death in the bowels of Ahab's palace was a very real possibility. He had heard the stories of how Ahab and Jezebel had treated Yahweh's few remaining prophets. They had been run through with the sword. What would it feel like, sharp metal ploughing through flesh, with mocking guards the last sound in your ears as life drained from you? Or perhaps death would be a saviour, mercifully snatching him from the hands of grinning torturers; blackness silencing his screams.

Hurriedly, Elijah shook off the clammy grip of fear and the horrifying images that crouched in a corner of his mind. He continued his walk, the royal city ever closer.

*   *   *

What kind of a man is it who can look death in the face and grin? Elijah was no Jonah—a reluctant prophet dragged by the Spirit kicking and screaming finally to speak for God. He knew the dangers and still made the trip. Such a man demands our attention.

We reveal volumes about ourselves when we open our mouths. Out of the abundance of the heart the mouth speaks. A lot of Elijah's personality and character is revealed by the few sentences that he speaks to the King. I imagine that he had agonised over his message, every word scrutinised in prayer until it became, as one commentator puts it, 'a spiritual stun grenade'.

'As the Lord, the God of Israel lives, whom I serve, there will be neither dew nor rain in the next few years except at my word.'

Elijah: man of truth and confrontation

Elijah was not reluctant to speak out in the most confrontational manner. He had no false commitment to bland niceness that some folk mistake for love. He was bold—and brief. Prophets have an ability to say a great deal with just a few hand-picked words. Nathan muttered just one sentence: 'You are the man!' and King David came tumbling down from his royal high horse; his scheming and adultery instantly under the prophetic spotlight.

Elijah makes no attempt at introduction or explanation—this isn't an occasion for subtlety or tact—so his words sting. They are a shocking slap in the royal face: 'In the name of Yahweh, the living God of Israel.' In the face of the Baal epidemic, Yahwehism had become something of an outdated tradition. At best it was a doctrine from the past—only around 7,000 people in the whole nation were still faithful to Yahweh—so the consensus was that Yahweh was dead, and the Baals lived. A succession of Israel's kings had mocked Yahweh by their lifestyles, words and flirtations with occultism. The fact that Yahweh had failed to respond with strategically directed lightning bolts, or indeed any other act of retribution, fuelled the notion that he no longer existed. 'Not so!' says Elijah. 'Yahweh is alive.' And the inference is obvious: 'The Baals are the lifeless ones around here.

They are images that can't see or hear; wooden godlings compared to the living God.'

In many ways, modern society mirrors the 'Where has God gone?' attitude of the ancients. While writing this chapter, a well-known international evangelist was interviewed live on BBC breakfast television, because of a major mission which was to take place in London in the next few days. The evangelist in question is a fairly controversial figure, but I was interested to note the look of total disbelief and wide-eyed astonishment on the interviewer's face—and all because the Christian leader made the comment, 'God spoke to me.'

'Excuse me,' interrupted the man from the BBC. 'Did you say . . . God speaks to you?'

'Certainly,' was the reply.

'You mean . . . God speaks to you?'

'Absolutely.'

The camera zoomed onto the face of the interviewer to capture his expression. It was a look that smugly declared, 'Oh boy, have I got one here.'

It seems God is allowed to exist as long as he doesn't speak, act, heal, or do anything else to interfere. 'If God isn't dead, then let him remain distant,' is the prevailing attitude. And anyone who suggests that God is a directly active deity obviously needs a psychiatric check-up.

Vague mysticism is in vogue. If you say, 'I love Jesus,' you're weird. If you announce to your friends that you begin each day by standing naked on your head and singing canticles to an Equadorian fruit bat by the name of 'Doris the winged one', then you're hip!

I think we can safely assume that Elijah would have treated the Christian liberals and the New Age 'truth is whatever you want it to be' philosophy that plagues contemporary society with an equal amount of tactless scorn and derision. In a world where, as Gerald Coates puts it, 'uncertainty is fashionable', we could use a few more prophets who are sure of their message and their God!

So, having nailed his colours to the mast, Elijah drives his point deeper, for not only is Yahweh the God who lives, but he is the real God of Israel. No wonder Jezebel had a fit. In the midst of a nationwide occult revival, Elijah plants a claim flag for God, who is not only the Lord of hosts, but the God of Israel too. He is the one who entered into covenant with Abraham and Moses, the real owner of the land. The message was plain—'Ahab! Your gods are dead impostors—lifeless squatters!'

Elijah left Ahab in absolutely no doubt as to the reality of the situation, and with a few words of clear confrontation made the position crystal clear. Of course, lest some take this act of anointed bluntness as a licence to be rude and arrogant in Jesus' name, we'd do well to remember that Elijah stood unswervingly on the word that God had placed in his heart, and not on his own opinions and prejudices.

Elijah: a man who knew who he was in God

'As the Lord, the God of Israel lives, whom I serve, there will be neither dew nor rain for the next few years, except at my word.'

Elijah knew who God was—and he knew who he was too. Humanly speaking, he was an obscure nobody from the hills of Gilead; a country bumpkin without the benefit of social pedigree or standing. Scruffy in his peasant's garb, prophesying to a man dripping gold and bedecked in the finest clothes, he could have so easily shrivelled with intimidation, a little man hopelessly out of his league. And let's be clear—Elijah was just a man. Some Jewish tradition suggests that Elijah was an angel, for only an extra-terrestrial could have done the exploits he did. Such a suggestion is theft, for this is a story of God being glorified through human weakness, water turned to wine, the ordinary becoming sacred. 'Elijah was a man just like us,' declares James (Jas 5:17).

However, he was a man with a sense of God-given identity, which had nothing to do with social climbing or designer clothing. He was the servant of the Lord, who, as one translator puts it, 'stood before God'. So he stood before two kings: one, a powerful but pathetic imitation of manhood; the other, the King of kings and Lord of lords, a powerful friend to have around when you're dancing with death! Only a man secure in his own identity could deliver the message that Elijah brought, which would have infuriated Ahab at every level. The weather forecast itself was bad—very bad! For three-and-a-half years the 'sky was shut up' as Jesus himself later described it. That was a massive blow for prosperous, thriving Israel. Even Ahab's political marriage to Jezebel from powerful Tyre couldn't save the nation from the famine that was to follow. There were other implications too. Many regarded Baal as the god of the sun—and so it was as if Elijah was saying, 'You want Baal and his sunshine, do you? Well, you'll get what you're craving for—non-stop!' Yet Baal worshippers believed that Baal controlled the rain as well and was responsible for abundant crops—so the message was doubly damning.

And then his final phrase was almost certainly guaranteed to send Ahab into a major fit, as Elijah announced: 'The sky is shut—until *I* open it!' What a slap in the royal face—a little man dressed in camel skins declaring: 'Yahweh is the real King, and I'm his prime minister, so there!'

If we are going to live lives of confidence, we had better get hold of the truth that God has called and invested us with a 'grace identity'. We too are the servants of God.

We often call ourselves names. Useless. Inconsistent. Weak. God calls us names too. Salt. Light. Overcomers. Chosen. Justified. Royal. Beloved. Friends of his. Children of the Father.

These are more than precious thoughts, pretty bouquets from a sentimental God. They form the backbone of our confidence. Sadly, we frequently forget who we are and become, as Michael Griffiths would put it, like 'Cinderella with amnesia', the bride who doesn't remember her name or to whom she is betrothed! Identity amnesia brings weakness and creeping paralysis. The God of Covenant found a bunch of half-starved Hebrew slaves who were being treated like scum by their Egyptian oppressors, and decided to give them a new name: 'Chosen'. Within a few weeks they forgot their new name and dubbed themselves with a lesser title: 'grasshoppers'. ('We seemed like grasshoppers in our own eyes, and we looked the same to [our enemies]'—Num 13:33.) If their choice of name seems ridiculous, then remember that there are many Christians today who feel it's very spiritual to denigrate themselves 'for God's glory'. I've winced my way through many a prayer meeting when the 'Oh Lord, we are but a bunch of mere slugs for thee, just verrucas in thy sight' type prayers were offloaded, it seemed, by the sackload. Robert Schuller has repeatedly pointed out that, as a group, evangelical Christians consistently rate lowest in the self-esteem polls. If we're not careful, we can become Christianised versions of the man in Jean-Paul Sartre's

The Flies who cries out: 'I stink! Oh, how I stink! I am a mass of rottenness! . . . I have sinned a thousand times. . . . and I reek to heaven!'*

Of course there is someone who is more than willing to help with our little renaming ceremonies: Satan is the enemy of identity. 'This is my Son, whom I love,' shouts the Father from heaven as Jesus allows John to push him under the water—identity affirmed. 'If you're the Son of God, do some magic tricks,' whispers the devil a couple of weeks later—identity questioned and denied. So expert is the enemy in the 'wagging finger—who's a piece of junk then?' department that Scripture describes him as the 'accuser of the brothers'. So much is accusation a part of his personality that his very name 'devil' comes from a root word meaning 'to accuse'. Satan shouts loudly too— the Greek word for accuser means 'one who speaks before a public tribunal'. No wonder so many Christians seem to drag themselves along the pathway of faith, weighed down with guilt and self-doubt. An expert lawyer for the prosecution (who has been in the business for quite a while, and knows all the tricks) is on their case! No wonder John Newton prayed:

> Be Thou my shield and hiding place
> That, sheltered near Thy side,
> I may my fierce accuser face,
> And tell him Thou hast died.

Unlike us, Elijah couldn't look back to a crucified, resurrected Jesus of history, and find his 'grace identity' there—but he knew that the hand of God was upon him. So, without apology, he stood before the King and Queen.

---

* Jean-Paul Sartre, *No Exit and Three Older Plays* (New York: Random House [Vintage Books], 1948), p 77.

Great things can be done by those who know who they
are—and who God is!

*   *   *

So Elijah strode into the royal courts, and fired his prophetic Exocet, which was greeted by stunned silence. The
royal servants knew better than to speak; they just stood
there, frozen by the moment, their own breathing loud in
their ears. Even the courtiers, Ahab's advisors and friends,
were stunned into silence, fearful of the King's face. His
eyes were cloudy, his face drained of blood, and he was
staring at the ground. After a few seconds that seemed like
hours, Ahab looked up, his eyes clear now, sharp with
anger, darting around the crowd.

And then they realised: the little man from the country
was gone.

3

Shaped for Significance: Junior School

> Then the word of the Lord came to Elijah: 'Leave here, turn
> eastward and hide in the Kerith Ravine, east of the Jordan.
> You will drink from the brook, and I have ordered the ravens
> to feed you there.' So he did what the Lord had told him. He
> went to the Kerith Ravine, east of the Jordan, and stayed there
> (1 Kings 17:2–5).

He was determined not to run. To run would undermine
the statement; it would give the impression that his confidence in God had only been a momentary thing, a
suicidal outburst at best. But now that the job was done,
it seemed like the adrenalin that had been pumping around
his body was draining swiftly, and as he walked quickly
away, merging into the crowd now, he realised that he
hadn't the faintest idea what he should do next. There had
been no arrest, no sharp order barked at the royal guards to
take him to the cells. There had been . . . nothing. So now
what?

It wasn't that he searched hard and long for the answer.
God took the initiative, because 'the word of the Lord
came to him'. As he hurried along as fast as decorum and
expediency would allow, he suddenly recognised that
voice he had come to trust, so much so that he had risked
his life to obey its commands, gently but clearly spoken
over the months.

Perhaps it seemed ridiculous; surely now was the time for Elijah to tour the nation, repeating the prophetic word of judgement to all who would listen. Or perhaps he should stay in Samaria and make himself available if by chance the King decided to respond to God's word and repent. But the voice was firm: 'Leave here!'

Quickly he came to the edge of the city, and turned eastward.

*　　*　　*

God appears to have a keen sense of irony. Elijah prophesies a lengthy drought, and then God speaks again and sends him off to a place called Cherith. There's double irony here, in that Cherith was a brook, and brooks are quick to dry up. A river would have been a more logical choice. To add potential insult to injury, the name 'Cherith' means 'drought' according to one commentator. 'Elijah, you've prophesied drought . . . so now head towards . . . drought!'

So what was God up to? Elijah was suddenly snatched off stage almost as soon as he had made his first dramatic entrance, and was destined to be parked by the brook for a long time. Why? Was it just that Elijah needed to hide away from Jezebel's roving assassins? After all, to be a prophet of Yahweh was to invite execution, and a number of the prophets had gone into hiding as a result. Obadiah was the chief steward of Ahab's palace, and enjoyed a place of prominence, more like a Prime Minister than a butler. An ancient seal has been found with the words, 'To Obadiah, servant of the King' written on it, and some scholars think it refers to the same man. He was a highly-placed mole, a spy for God, who was indeed 'servant of the King', but (as the name Obadiah declares in the Hebrew) he was the 'servant of Yahweh' too. This faithful man had worshipped the true God since his youth, and now he personally undertook a rescue mission for the prophets, hiding 100 of them in two caves, providing food and water for them from the palace stocks (Ahab and Jezebel were unwittingly feeding the prophets of Baal and Yahweh at the same time). So perhaps we could be forgiven for thinking that God was providing a hiding place for Elijah until Jezebel's temper cooled, particularly as the English translation of 1 Kings 17 includes the word 'hide'.

Not so! Elijah was never called to hide in the conventional sense of the word. Indeed, when Jezebel issued a personal death threat sometime later in Elijah's life, and the prophet took things into his own hands and ran away, God sent him straight back into the situation. No, the *safety* of Elijah wasn't the primary motivation for the trip to Cherith—but the *shaping* of Elijah was.

God's strategy for developing character: shaping

We've already taken a look at some of the foundations of Elijah's life in the previous chapter, but foundations aren't enough. Even though Elijah had responded with commendable faithfulness and obedience to his first mission, there was still a great deal of shaping and further preparation needed before he could stand on Mount Carmel and take on the prophets of Baal. One success didn't mean that graduation day had arrived.

Greatness, as the Bible defines it, never comes suddenly. It is normally forged in the furnace of time. Before

Moses could lead the Hebrews out of Egypt, he had to spend forty years in Pharaoh's palace learning to be a somebody, then forty years as a man on the run learning to be a nobody, and then the last forty years leading the people of God, discovering that God uses nobodies.

David spent a lot of his early days watching sheep—hardly the most exciting lifestyle. But the Good Shepherd was around too, and was continually investing in David's character during those long hot days and cold nights, preparing him for the greatness that was to come. Peter had to sit by the fire with Jesus and find out just how much he really loved his Master before he could preach his first sermon or discover the healing power of God pulsating from his own shadow.

The reason for the shaping process is simple. God is more interested in the character of his children than he is in their gifting.

So, even though Elijah was flushed with success, it was nevertheless school time for him, and the junior school was called Cherith. Before we go any further, we need to forget any ideas of the exiled prophet sitting by a beautiful, crystal-clear stream, enjoying fabulous scenery and having a party with his Maker, another day in paradise as the water bubbled and sang. Cherith was an ugly place, where a small seep of water had worn away rock and stone to gouge out a stark, deep gash in the desert. And the water wasn't exactly Perrier! It would have been muddy and murky and dotted with debris. The weather was hot—often 120 degrees in the afternoon—which would have helped the growth of thick, green algae. Far from being rested in an idyllic resort, Elijah was holed up in the back end of the desert—and forced to sip scum soup in order to survive.

Four character lessons for budding prophets and 'Baal-busters'

1. Believers, live your beliefs

Elijah had *spoken* God's judgement—now he had to flesh it out with prophetic action. When God told the prophet, 'Hide yourself!' he used a term which would be more accurately translated as 'absent yourself'. The same Hebrew word is used in Genesis 31:49: 'May the Lord keep watch between you and me when we *are away from each other.'*

God didn't call Elijah to run away. Rather, his exit was a dramatic sign of God's displeasure, an acted-out shout from Yahweh: 'Judgement has come, and my man, my representative, is hereby *outa here!*' Prophecy is more than words. Some of the most powerful prophetic moments I have ever witnessed have been dramatic—a hammer methodically tapping a milk bottle; a person lifted into the air, held up by their friends. Jeremiah threw pots around. Ezekiel made scale models of cities and then lay on his side for about thirteen months (and then, by way of a change, rolled over to the other side for another six weeks). Micah took all his clothes off and went around naked to prove a prophetic point. And Agabus, a leading prophet in the early church, prophesied Paul's forth-coming imprisonment by tying him up with a belt.

This, however, was more than an act of drama: Elijah was being called to live with the implications of his own message, even though it cost him dearly. Admittedly, God sent him to a familiar place, for Tishbe was on the Cherith, and so it was most likely Elijah's youthful stomping ground. He would have played in this area as a child. But there was still a cost, because now he had to live outside the warmth of the community of family and friends, alone with God.

He had spoken the word. Now he had to live the word. The challenge to us is obvious: as Christians we must continually ensure that we are living by truth as well as believing it, lest we fall into 'believism'—the idea that intellectual adherence to a body of truth is sufficient. James warns us about being deceived by the idea that *hearing* the word is enough (Jas 1:22), and all Christians, particularly preachers, need to know that to *preach and proclaim* the word is not enough either. Perhaps that is why some leaders fall into gross sin and then end up preaching an endless series of messages on the very sin they are privately indulging in. The recent scandal of a TV evangelist who consorted with prostitutes over a long period, but also wrote books condemning the evils of pornography and preached his hardest and hottest sermons on sexual sin, is a case in point. Ted Engstrom's words sting: 'It's dishonest to talk about the power of prayer and lead a prayerless life. Isn't it dishonest to talk about forgiveness and fail to forgive?'*

Living the message starts with the so-called small issues. We may not be guilty of armed robbery, but are we paying our bills on time? An appointment with a prostitute may be a million miles from our thinking, but what do we watch on TV late at night, when we've worked hard and 'just need to relax . . .'?

Bill Hybels is the dynamic leader of the 20,000-strong Willow Creek Community Church near Chicago, and his ministry has recently gained increasing profile in Europe.

---

* Ted Engstrom, *Integrity* (Waco, Texas: Word, 1987), p 92.

God has trusted Hybels with a great anointing. Read his words here and you'll understand why.

One evening, I stopped by the church just to encourage those who were rehearsing there for the Spring Musical. I didn't intend to stay long so I parked my car next to the entrance. After a few minutes I ran back to my car and drove home.

The next morning I found a note in my office mail box. It read: 'A small thing, but Tuesday night when you came to rehearsal you parked in the "No Parking" area. A reaction from one of my crew (who did not recognise you after you got out of your car) was, "There's another jerk in the 'No Parking' area!" We try hard not to allow people—even workers—to park anywhere other than the parking lot. I would appreciate your co-operation too.' It was signed by a member of our maintenance staff.

This man's stock went up in my book because he had the courage to write to me about what could have been a slippage in my character. And he was right on the mark. As I drove up that night I had thought, 'I shouldn't park here, but after all, I am the Pastor.' That translates 'I am an exception to the rules'. But that employee wouldn't allow me to sneak down the road labelled 'I am an exception'. I am not the exception to Church rules or any of God's rules. As a leader I am not an exception: I'm to be the example. According to scripture I am to live in such a way that I can say 'Follow me. Park where I park. Live as I live.'*

* Bill Hybels, 'But I'm an exception' (*Leadership Magazine*: Spring 1988, vol 9, no 2), p 37.

2. Remember that we are all called to serve God in a sphere of his choosing

'The best way to create a good, healthy self-image is to be honest about self-definition. I would like to sing, but I can't.' So says Steve Brown.*

Elijah was called to what seemed to be a quick retirement. After all, one national prophecy in three years is hardly a heavy caseload. But at this period of his life, his sphere, or arena of operation, was the delivery of just one single-sentence sermon. He could have travelled as an itinerant revivalist, but that wasn't his sphere. He could have joined the prophetic school, brought some leadership to that group, and taken care of them—but that was Obadiah's task, and not part of Elijah's job description at this time, although he would get involved with schools later. Like Elijah we need to have a sober, rational assessment of our gifting, so that while we do develop and grow, we don't step out way beyond it.

Of course, spheres are flexible; they expand and change, and sometimes God completely changes our sphere of operation, so we shouldn't get too locked up in them. However, an understanding of our sphere helps us to respond appropriately to opportunities that come our way. There are some things that I know I should never do—singing, for example! I used to sing in a Christian rock band, but all aspirations in that direction ended because I became increasingly aware that when I sang people cried out to God—and not in repentance!

I also know there are some things that are not part of my *primary* calling which I may nevertheless occasionally

---

* Steven Brown, '13 Fatal Errors Managers Make' in *Don't Let Them Sit on You* (Kingsway, 1988).

give myself to. When you are clear about your calling, you can rejoice at the successes of others and avoid feelings of jealousy or insecurity, because you know that you are secure in what you do, and that God has called others to function differently.

One word of warning about spheres: we shouldn't use this kind of talk as an excuse to avoid doing the things that we all find tedious. 'I can't stack the chairs or pick up a piece of litter after the meeting, because it's not my calling or sphere.' We do well to remember that we never leave the sphere of servanthood, whatever our arena of operation.

3. God is full of surprises

God had made all the catering arrangements for Elijah, but his methods were somewhat unusual—he was to be fed twice each day by a flock of ravens.

Some commentators rebel at the idea of God commanding a squadron of birds to feed a prophet: one says that the word for 'ravens' (*haorebim*) is similar to the word for 'Arabs' (*haarabim*), so therefore it was Bedouins who fed the exiled Elijah, rather than birds. I'll leave Old Testament scholar James Battenfield to deal with that little piece of fancy footwork: 'This [Arab] idea unnecessarily takes much of the miraculous out of the account and is not based on any versional support. Elijah has seen Yahweh's miraculous provision.'

Even the birds of the air obey the commands of the Lord. But don't be tempted to romanticise the scene—grinning birds landing in perfect formation, each dropping their piece of sirloin steak onto a silver platter marked with an 'X' in the middle like a helicopter pad, as Elijah tucks his napkin into his collar and picks up his knife and fork. . . .

Of course, there were practical reasons for God hiring a bunch of bird-caterers. While we've already established that Elijah wasn't hiding in the conventional sense of the word, none the less there still might have been the odd bounty hunter out looking to make a fast shekel out of presenting Elijah's head to Ahab and Jezebel. If Obadiah (or perhaps one of God's 7,000 faithful still living in Israel) had been given the catering contract, they may have been followed by a would-be hit-man. But birds are impossible to follow—and besides, what suspicion would be stirred by the sight of a bunch of ravens flying by with food in their beaks? Quite apart from the aspect of security, the provision from the ravens must have been a source of encouragement to the lonely prophet-in-exile. Twice a day he was reminded that God was supernaturally involved in every detail of his life.

However, there was another reason for this rather bizarre arrangement. Elijah obviously had to learn that God is full of variety and surprise. Passionate believers fall quickly into the trap of legalism, so it was time for Elijah to learn that God was no sterile, do-things-by-the-book type deity. Thus Elijah ends up with a bird as a maître'd!

He probably groaned at the thought—the possibility of being drip-fed from a bird beak wasn't exciting. Ravens feed on offal, carrion and rotting matter generally—they love to hang around rubbish tips. And now those very same beaks were under divine orders.

And weren't ravens designated as unclean according to the Law? Elijah may have frantically searched his memory. What was it the Law said? 'These are the birds you are to detest and not eat because they are detestable: the eagle, the vulture, the black vulture, the red kite, any kind of black kite, *any kind of raven*' (Lev 11:13–15, italics mine).

Technically, the Law wasn't being broken, because Elijah wasn't eating the birds; they were just playing waiter. But even so, what was God up to? Yahweh was teaching his servant that he will not be locked in by preconceived ideas or legalistic straightjackets.

When it comes to the things that God wants to do, the past is often the enemy of the present—especially if the past was blessed by the kiss of revival. I have met so many people who genuinely experienced the power of God during the Pentecostal revival that took place both in Britain and the USA at the beginning of this century, many of whom are bitterly opposed to what God is doing today. Why?

Why is it that the radicals who historically rode the crest of yesterday's revival are so often the opponents of the next wave? The answer can be summed up in one word: inflexibility. We get focused on the *style* in which God moved, and the methods that he blessed yesterday. We then get suspicious when, because God is moving on and is the author of freshness and creativity, he decides to do something utterly new which shatters all of our preconceived ideas. 'That's not *real* revival,' we mutter.

Of course the danger is as real for those of us who consider ourselves to be radicals in the 1990s. Will we get stuck in our brand new ruts, arch-defenders of the house-group system/forty-five minutes of soft rock type worship/three prophecies, a picture and a reading or two/ march up and down and rebuke the principality over Cuba approach? Will we be guilty of trumpeting yesterday's tired old themes, forcing God to pass us by and raise up a fresh generation of radicals?

There were to be lots of surprising twists and turns

ahead as Elijah followed God, and the flying food force helped the prophet prepare for the unexpected—though I doubt whether Elijah realised that when he was woken up each morning by a large flock of ravens spitting their offerings at his feet.

4. He who would shout must first learn to be still

It was such a sudden transformation. One moment he was standing in the presence of the King of the land; now he was breakfasting with winged scavengers. The day before he'd squeezed through the bustling crowds of the city, senses stirred by the noises and the smells of a relative metropolis; now, only the relentless but gentle bubbling of the brook.

No time to be swung up onto the shoulders of Yahweh's faithful, a new folk hero who had taken on the King himself. No pats on the back, no warm smiles and 'well dones'.

Just water. Those birds again. And God.

Perhaps it's hard for us in our frantic, addicted-to-activity society to relate to this scene. Most of us feel that the urgent jangling of the alarm clock is really like a starter's pistol to the beginning of every hurried day. The moment our feet hit the floor they land on a fast-moving conveyor belt—things to do, places to go, people to see, life in the fast lane, busy, busy. . . .

Even our leisure has a frantic feel about it. Theme parks provide us with the latest stomach-churning 'happening'. We don't want to relax. We want to see, touch, feel everything! Turn on the TV. Rent a video. Listen to a CD (go on, I like it *loud* . . .). Save planet earth from certain destruction in the privacy of your front room via your Nintendo game.

And so stillness becomes something to avoid. Silence is

our enemy. The jogger out in the beautiful countryside plugs his brain into the Walkman. Never mind the hum of nature and the sound of the breeze in the long grass, give me other sounds. . . .

Phone the doctor. You're on hold, but don't worry. We'll play you music, lest you should have to endure twenty seconds or so of . . . silence.

Applaud the man who works a seven-day week (ninety hours or so they say), who works out in order to maintain efficiency, who listens to subliminal teaching tapes about increasing productivity while he sleeps . . . and who dies of a heart attack at the age of forty-three, slumped in the arms of the wife whom he didn't get to know that well . . . there wasn't time.

And then we stop just long enough to ask a man who goes by the name Prince of Peace to take charge of our lives. But on we race, keep up the pace, pound the treadmill. Not much has changed, only now we go to the meeting on Sunday, house group on Wednesday, evangelism on Saturday morning. . . .

The gentle murmuring of the brook seems a million miles away from where we're at in the 1990s. 'It's all right for you, Elijah, but life's not like that now.' And, in many ways, that's true. The idea of dropping out for a while remains an elusive dream for most of us. So what are we to do? After all, stillness must be a priority. In the original Hebrew, when God directs Elijah to Cherith, there is a strong emphasis that says: 'I'll meet your needs, Elijah—but I'll meet them there.' Cherith was non-negotiable.

Perhaps we can begin by learning to build stillness in the midst of busyness. You can't get away from it all for a month or maybe even two days—but you can for ten minutes. Leave a book in the bathroom so that you can take a five-minute study vacation when you visit the smallest room. (Be careful that you don't park there for hours because you got too engrossed in the book—this will not bless the other members of your household!) Ignore the crowded lift and climb the stairs. Remember the television comes fitted with an off button. Write a few scriptures on a piece of paper, stick it on the fridge, and stop once in a while to read and think about them.

Deliberately slow down. I do a great deal of travelling, and my tendency is to work out just exactly how long it will take me to get to a place, and then go screaming down the motorway with foot pulverising the accelerator . . . at 69.9999 miles per hour of course.

Breathless but triumphant, I arrive having shaved a whole ten minutes off my previous land speed record. This great feat was accomplished by my refusing to stop for petrol. To do so would have wasted a precious five minutes. The downside of this decision is that I've been driving perilously close to empty; thus most of the trip has been spent with my back arched with tension over the steering wheel and my eyes darting towards the petrol gauge every seventeen seconds, as I quickly overtake in order to save another few moments.

The other night, however, I tried my Cherith experiment. I left half an hour earlier for my speaking engagement, and took the country lanes rather than the motorway. I decided to take my time, enjoy the scenery and chat with God. I'm sorry to report that no land speed records were broken—but I arrived at my destination relaxed, refreshed and raring to go. Strange as it may seem, you can install a brook into your car!

I have some friends in America who are passionate about astronomy. Apparently their best star-gazing experiences take place when they pack their equipment into their car and drive a few miles out of town. They have to get away from the upward glare of the city lights in order to focus on what's above. Of course, the stars are always there—it's just that the fluorescent glare of the streets shrouds them from view.

God is there, but often he is made distant by the glare of our feverish living. Stillness allows us to turn down the lights, and zoom in on him for a while.

Perhaps, like me, you'd like a real Mount Carmel type faith: mighty miracles, bold confidence, fearless faith. The story of Elijah shows us that there is a road to Carmel. It passes through Cherith.

4

High School: Zarephath

Then the word of the Lord came to him: 'Go at once to Zarephath of Sidon and stay there. I have commanded a widow in that place to supply you with food' (1 Kings 17:8–9).

God's man or woman is early selected and slowly educated for the job.*

Elijah had been about a year by the brook now, but he had learned a lifetime's lessons. Perhaps at first curiosity had nibbled away at him: what was going on in the big city? Had there been a change of heart from the King—or was Elijah now Israel's most wanted man? But as the weeks went by, the questions diminished as the encouraging voice seemed to boom in the Cherith silence. One thing was beyond doubt—God was taking care of him; the clockwork arrival of the ravens 700 times over assured him of that.

God has no graduates in his university. The process of learning and shaping is continuous, and from a human perspective, God seems to be in no hurry. Kosuke

---

* Søren Kierkegaard, *Attack upon Christendom* (Princeton, NJ: Princeton University Press, 1968), p 195.

Koyama writes in *The Three Mile an Hour God* that God works at the speed a person walks—and we may well find his pace painstakingly slow. Koyama uses the 'Wilderness College course' in which the Hebrews were 'enrolled' as an example: 'Forty years for one lesson! How slow, and how patient! No university can run on this basis . . . God goes slowly in His educational process of man. Forty years in the wilderness points to his basic educational policy.'*

It was time for the next stage in the prophet's development: Zarephath.

*   *   *

Zarephath! There were plenty of very good reasons why it was the last place to go. First of all, it was in the opposite direction from Samaria; now he would be further away from the action. It was about eighty miles away, a hefty trek. More significantly, however, it was in a foreign country—and just eight miles down the coast from Jezebel's home city of Tyre.

Then, to top it all, the man who had been supernaturally provided for twice a day would from now have to rely on the charity of an impoverished widow—who is most likely not a follower of Yahweh. No chance for pride to settle in this heart ('Let me tell you about the year of 700 miracles . . . '). Any thoughts of writing an exciting testimony book *With the Ravens at the Ritz* go out of the window, because

---

* Kosuke Koyama, *The Three Mile an Hour God* (London: SCM, 1979), pp 3, 6–7.

God puts Elijah on welfare. It may have seemed like an ironic joke on God's part, for in a time of scorching drought, God sends him from Cherith ('drought') to Zarephath ('smelting furnace'). While wishing to avoid lame analogies about refining fire, God turning the temperature up, and all that, I think you'll agree that there is a certain irony in it all, as Elijah trudges eighty sunbaked miles to a divinely appointed oven. Who says the road to greatness and glory is easy?

*   *   *

Hunger had gouged her face; stark hollows where cheeks should have been, sucked in now by malnutrition. Her skin, once smooth and lovely, had been folded deep with creases by the sharp edge of poverty. Her hair hung lank over bony shoulders, and her arms and legs were pathetic spindles, impossibly fragile. But it was her eyes that told the story. They were cold and bleak; she was a dead woman walking. Life had been nothing more than a day-to-day fight for existence for as long as she could remember. With her husband long gone, she had been left to fend for herself, and now even her son was too weak to do the basic chores. As she scurried around by the city gates, perhaps she remembered better days, when her husband gossiped and laughed there with the other men of the city, their voices echoing around the walls as darkness closed in at the end of the day. But that was all a very long time ago. Now, there was nothing left, and no chance of better days.

For some while she had felt some vague hope; a

persistent thought had been nagging at her mind for weeks: 'A man comes.'

A man comes. From God.

Probably just wishful thinking—or maybe a premonition about the angel of death, coming for her and her bag-of-bones son. It was time to let hope die, and life with it. One last meal then, and afterwards perhaps the gods would be merciful and let them die in their sleep. . . .

*　　*　　*

Perhaps he caught sight of her as he sat by the city gate, exhausted by the five-day journey, wondering what to do next. He would have felt the agony that was written all over her, maybe even wavered for a moment about that prayer for drought cried out so long ago. In a way, even though the thought was perverse, he was partially responsible for her pain. He watched her scrabbling around for a few sticks to make an evening fire, conscious of that nervous gnawing that comes from being a stranger in a foreign land.

And then he realised. It was her.

*　　*　　*

Put yourself in Elijah's sandals for a few moments. You're tired, hungry, and probably somewhat desperate for some human company after a year in isolation. Warmly assured that God has got everything organised, you've emigrated, though there is some concern as you are now in pagan territory mainly inhabited by Baal worshippers.

You're looking forward to your first meal provided by human hands in over twelve months—and you discover that God's provision is a very confused and undernourished woman with suicidal tendencies. Perhaps Elijah looked around the city square and noticed some other more well-to-do ladies with a good deal more flesh on their bones and hope in their hearts. Why couldn't it be one of them whom he was to stay with?

If I had been in his position, I would have been tempted to look elsewhere, especially when God had said, 'I have commanded a widow to sustain you,' and then, when Elijah asks for food, she says that she doesn't have enough and that this is her funeral meal anyway! With a slight cough of embarrassment, I would have heartily apologised for my stupid error of mistaken identity and, with a sigh of relief, beat a very hasty retreat. But not Elijah.

The circumstances seem to contradict what God has said. 'I'm providing for you at Zarephath,' says God, and Elijah finds himself staring at abject poverty and death—hardly a comforting confirmation. But something else begins to ring in his mind as the woman describes her empty bowl and jar.

Prophets are often triggered by the sight of objects which seem to suggest a divine truth. Like a prophetic litany, a repetitive chant, words begin to form in Elijah's mind. Lance Pierson suggests they were formed in compressed, rhythmic form:

> Jar of meal will not be spent,
> Jug of oil will not be emptied,
> Till I Yahweh send the rain . . .

A prophetic rap from God.

Quickly he assures the woman that all will be well, and asks her to prepare a meal. The black and white portrait then begins to burst into colour as a miracle blossoms. For 'many days' the food is miraculously provided. The supernatural has restored laughter and hope to a widow's home once again, and Baal gets a slap in the face too. An ancient stele has been found portraying Baal holding a spear which contains a plant or a tree. One of his many names was 'Baal ben Dagan' (Son of Dagan), and 'Dagan' means corn. This particular Baal was therefore supposed to be a vegetation god, whose blessing was needed for plentiful corn. Many scholars believe that it was Baal Dagan that was the principal deity in Sidon. And now Elijah multiplies the corn—in the name of Yahweh.

Zarephath was a place of strategically significant miracles—true signs and wonders, supernatural acts that declared truth—and furthermore, for Elijah, school was very much back in session.

A few more lessons for heroes in the making

1. What you are at home and in close relationships is what you really are

Elijah emerges from Cherith with a briefcase full of life lessons learned, but now he has to learn to live out those discoveries in the rough and tumble of a family life. It has been said that 'religion is what a person does with solitude'. While there is a measure of truth in that statement, it isn't the whole truth. I find it quite easy to be massively spiritual when I'm alone. I'm blessed to live in Sussex, and really enjoy going out to pray on the glorious South Downs. It's easy to be very holy while walking along with the warm sunshine on my back, quietly singing or praying or thinking about Scripture. For me, religion in solitude is the easy part. The difficulty is working all that wonderful spirituality out at home when my children are practising the violin at 7am and I'm awakened by what sounds like a number of animals being systematically strangled.

It's easy to be politely gracious and self-sacrificing at the Sunday meeting—but slightly more challenging when you're deeply engrossed in a political documentary and your children are pleading with you to switch channels to the cartoons so that they can admire their favourite duck.

I'm certainly humbled by Catherine Bramwell-Booth's description of her Salvation Army Father, Bramwell Booth: 'When he told us about Christ, told us Who He was and what He did, we understood. We felt . . . that our Father himself was like the Christ he loved.'*

I'm grateful that I'm not alone in being humbled and challenged to do better in this area. Prominent American politician and leading Christian, Senator Mark Hatfield confesses: 'The home is the toughest environment of all for leaders. Why is it that the ones we love the most are the ones that we are most impatient with? My wife has often said to me, "I wish you were as patient with your children as you are with your constituents."'†

Of course, it's not only leaders who are prone to suffer from this split personality spirituality. Tony Campolo wisely counsels young people:

---

* Catherine Bramwell-Booth, *Commissioner Catherine* (London: Darton, Longman and Todd, 1983), p 77.
† Harold Myra (ed), *Leaders* (Carol Stream, Ill: CTI Word, 1987), pp 52–53.

Sometimes, after Christian young people have been off to a church camp or religious weekend retreat, they come home 'talking the language of Zion' and, with pious platitudes, give testimonies of how their lives have been changed by God. However, none of this has any significance unless it changes the way they act at home. Those who have had genuine conversion experiences will give evidence of their new life in Christ by how they relate to their parents.*

Let us not be fooled into believing that our public behaviour represents who and what we really are—in that arena there exist all kinds of artificial constraints of propriety and performance. We are truly what we are in the home. The real us is to be most accurately measured by the jokes we tell as part of our 'let our hair down' friendships, rather than the fine biblical illustrations that flow from our lips on public platforms. And if, like me, you find that quite a daunting challenge, be encouraged by the fact that it was Elijah's family/home period that was called 'the smelting pot'.

It was American President Harry Truman who said, 'If you can't stand the heat, get out of the kitchen.' In this context, let us alter the saying to: 'If you can't stand the heat, then stay in the kitchen—you'll probably learn some fantastic lessons there!'

2. Personal rejection is often part of the Christian life

It's amazing how human beings have such short memories when it comes to God's blessing—and limited loyalty too. Israel marches across the dry ground that seconds earlier was the Red Sea. They then jump up and down, punch tambourines and yell the Hebrew equivalent of 'jolly good

---

* Tony Campolo, *Seven Deadly Sins* (Wheaton, Ill: Victor Books, 1987), p 57.

show' as God permanently water baptises the Egyptian army. . . and then start moaning and pining for Egypt in almost the same breath. The Hebrews displayed the remarkable human tendency quickly to forget what they should remember, and remember what they should forget.

This strategic amnesia is also in evidence at the trial of the Lord Jesus. Hearts which had swelled with the word 'Hosanna!' on Palm Sunday quickly switched tack and screamed, 'Crucify him!' The satanically inspired religious cheerleaders only succeeded in whipping the crowd into a bloodthirsty frenzy because of this human tendency quickly to forget the handiwork of God.

And now Elijah becomes a victim of this syndrome. For months he is the honoured and welcome guest in the widow's home—the man whom God sent, the agent of deliverance, the hero of the hour. But today's hero quickly becomes tomorrow's scapegoat when things go wrong. In the midst of a miracle, death comes as the widow's son falls sick and finally passes away. Suddenly, it's all Elijah's fault. Elijah represents Yahweh, so when the widow feels frustrated and angry with God, God's man gets it in the neck: 'What do you have against me, man of God? Did you come to remind me of my sin and kill my son?'

One moment Elijah is the man of the year, the next he's a murderer. Notice the widow seems quickly to connect the death of her boy with something evil that was in her past (though we don't know the details, she obviously had a skeleton or two hanging in her cupboard), but in her grief, she blasts Elijah with three unjustified bullets. The temptation for Elijah must have been to justify himself.

'You've got something against me.' ('What do you mean, lady? I've been happily living here and we've seen an amazing miracle every day.')

'You've reminded me of my sin.' ('I didn't say a
word.')

'You've killed my son.' ('I didn't do it—he's been sick
for a long time, as you well know. I've been praying for
him, and now what do I get? False accusations. Huh!')

3. Compassion is at the heart of every miracle

Elijah manfully avoids the 'nobody loves me, time to
begin a diet of worms' sulk. He ignores the false accusation (and the bad theology) that declared, 'This has happened because I've been naughty.' This wasn't the time
for personal defence or theological debate—the boy had
stopped breathing, and Elijah had come to love this
family. Now he learns to pray, not because of anger at
national occultism or righteous indignation—but because
he cares. Blazing passion for the law drove him to pray the
drought prayer; sobbing compassion for the grieving
drives him to raise the dead.

And driven he is! He certainly has a no-holds-barred
approach to the calamity. Boiling anger and frustration are
hurled at God himself: 'Then he cried out to the Lord, "O
Lord my God, have you brought tragedy also upon this
widow I am staying with, by causing her son to die?"' (1
Kings 17:20).

This is no passive 'if it be thy will, O God, then raise
this unfortunate up' speech. This is a crying heart opened
to heaven, a rage, even, that spills like a torrent as Elijah
looks at the whitening cold corpse on his bed. And then he
'stretches himself' upon the boy, not once, but three
times. How does a fully grown man 'stretch' his limbs
out on the small body of a child? Elijah literally covered
the child's body with his own. Some commentators suggest that he did so as if to say to God: 'Let my life be his
life, my breath be his breath. Take me rather than him.'

As he did so, yet another taboo bit the dust—the one about touching dead bodies: 'Whoever touches the dead body of anyone will be unclean for seven days' (Num 19:11).

The Jews regarded a corpse as exceptionally defiling—that's why the graves or sepulchres were 'whitened' so that they would be easily recognisable. But Elijah was prepared to go to any length, including making himself personally 'unclean'. It was the same kind of compassion that caused Jesus to touch the dead body of another widow's son hundreds of years later.

Compassion must be at the heart of any cry for the miraculous. God has no interest in providing Holy Spirit ignited fireworks for the delight and entertainment of the Christian public. He offers his power because he cares for people—and lest we be guilty of becoming like the sign-seekers who followed Jesus around, we need to ensure that our motive is the same, in everything we do for God. Evangelism without compassion is heartless expansionism.

4. Influence, both good and bad, is constantly ours

In this case, the story has a happy-ever-after ending. A beautiful reunion takes place as Elijah carries the now-living child downstairs and announces: 'Look! Your son is alive!' Notice there's not even a hint of self-praise in Elijah's words; no sense of, 'Wow! Look what happened when *I* prayed.' But the woman knows it is Elijah whom God has heard, and so is able to exclaim, 'Now I know that you are a man of God and that the word of the Lord from your mouth is the truth.' When Elijah and the widow first met, she referred to 'the Lord *your* God'—she was prepared to acknowledge his existence, but had no personal experience of him.

Now that's all changed, for she has seen truth, and that truth has been modelled in Elijah. Those who rub shoulders with the property of God run the risk of being changed for ever.

Paul Borthwick tells the story of missionary Gordon Maxwell:

> He went to India as a missionary, and his Christian conduct and commitment were evident to all. On one occasion, he asked a Hindu man to teach him the local language. The Hindu man replied, 'No, sahib, for you will convert me to Christianity.'
>
> Maxwell tried to clarify: 'You don't understand, all I want you to do is teach me the language.' But the Hindu replied, 'I will not, for no one can live with you and not become a Christian.'*

We are called to *be* good news, not just talk about it. That's why we're called salt and light, for both of these elements change and affect. Both disturb the status quo by their very existence and presence. Such knowledge should cause us to be careful, for as J.R. Miller says:

> There have been meetings of only a moment which have left impressions for life, for eternity. No one can understand that mysterious thing we call influence . . . yet . . . every one of us continually exerts influence, either to heal, to bless, to leave marks of beauty; or to wound, to hurt, to poison, to stain other lives.†

To live with Elijah was to discover that the God of Israel was lodging there too. And with that reality in place, Elijah came to the end of school. He had spent time in

* Paul Borthwick, *Leading the Way* (Colorado Springs: NavPress, 1989), p66.
† J.R. Miller, *The Building of Character*

solitude, and discovered a million truths about God and self there. He'd then lived those truths out in the challenging context of friendship and family. It had been a long and rigorous training course, and had demanded everything he had. Longfellow speaks the truth about greatness of character:

> The heights by great men reached and kept
> Were not attained by sudden flight,
> But they, while their companions slept,
> Were toiling upward in the night.

But while the education process had been tough, both Cherith and Zarephath were gentle hillsides compared with the mountain that Elijah was now called to climb.

That mountain was called Carmel.

5

Carmel

In Samaria, the man they called King sat alone, silent, thoughtful. The room in which he sat was splendid; every wall was breathtaking, panelled from floor to ceiling with intricately carved ivory; figures of lions, griffins and sphinxes stared down. The place overflowed with the trappings of royalty. Even the bed ends, table tops and chair backs were ivory-clad.

But Ahab had no eyes for such things now. His servants had been dismissed, scurrying away at his yell, bowing and retreating at the same time. They were used to these moods of his. Sometimes the King would shut himself away for days on end, and the servants knew well that to disturb him was to die.

The door shut now, he was alone with his thoughts— and fears.

How could it have come to this? Here he was, the King of Israel, a man who had known fabulous wealth and massive power. He had lived a life that other men could only dream about, with a sumptuous palace, beautifully decorated, no expense spared, a country house in Jezreel, and anything his heart desired.

The word of his command was backed up by 2,000 chariots and 10,000 men—the royal stables at Megiddo had been a pride and joy since Solomon's time. He had chosen to base himself in a fortified city that would provide the highest security confidence: Samaria was set on a hill 300 feet high. It was surrounded by two fortification walls—the outer wall nineteen feet thick, the inner wall five feet thick.

Good fortune had kissed his friends as well: Israel's upper classes had enjoyed long, luxurious years of prosperity. Of course, the peasant classes had suffered in order to pay for the few to live in luxury. Extortion and oppression were rife, but what of it? The poor were nothing—little people, expendable. Perhaps it was meant to be that way, the will of the gods. He smiled at the thought. That was it—the poor were victims by destiny. There was no need for concern or conscience. It was meant to be.

However, despite all that had been, the drought was now taking its toll. He'd heard about the scorched farms, brown and barren. Stories were circulating about the growing numbers of corpses that were to be seen lying in the fields, some crawling with corruption, others bleached white bones, poor pickings for the birds.

Samaria, the royal city, was suffering the worst effects of the drought. Curses! It was as if Yahweh had targeted him, singled him out for punishment—fine treatment for a man who had named his children in Yahweh's honour. . . .

Now his horses were dying. His servants would always find water for the palace, but over at Megiddo Stables they had encountered real problems with their supply, and now reports were coming in that those once beautiful, sleek animals were dropping like flies. So desperate had he been that he, the King, had taken his steward Obadiah out into the countryside on a secret mission to try to find grazing pasture, but the mission had been a failure.

Kicking his footstool aside, the King got up and walked to the window. How often the view from here had brought him pleasure. Looking eastward, he could see the rich hills of Gilead on the horizon.

Gilead was the home of that pious trouble-maker, Elijah. Four years ago, no one in the land had ever heard that cursed man's name. Back then he was just another worthless peasant, garbed in his crude camel skins. But now the common people were saying that it was Elijah who was really in charge of Israel: the wretched man had announced famine, and then disappeared out of sight. He hadn't been seen or heard of for years! Ambassadors had been sent out to all the surrounding nations, demanding that Elijah be extradited if he was living within their borders. Threats, pleas, bribes—nothing had worked.

Then, at Jezebel's suggestion, the last few remaining Yahweh prophets had been arrested and tortured, in the hope that they would provide some information. However, despite the unspeakable things that had been done to their bodies, none had talked. In the end, Jezebel had suggested that they all be put to death. After all, when the master of the lower chamber had finished with them, they were almost dead anyway, so why not just be rid of them and their irritating rantings for good? Jezebel. Clever Jezebel. His lovely wife, who always knew what to do.

Yet none of this had led to the discovery and arrest of Elijah. Perhaps, Ahab hoped, the obnoxious man was dead. Perhaps one of those whitened skeletons was all that was left of the man. . . . He smiled at the thought.

Suddenly, his moment of pleasure was shattered by a nervous tapping at the door. Hadn't he left strict orders? Furious, he span around from the window, spat out an obscenity and marched towards the door. Someone would die for this! The door opened, and Obadiah quickly bowed.

'News, your Majesty. It's the prophet . . . I mean, the

Tishbite. He's back—I spoke with him today. Sir . . . he
wants to see you.'

Ahab punched the air with rage, his teeth grinding with
frustration, death in his eyes. He, the King, was being
summoned by a fugitive peasant! The indignity, the
audacity . . . the. . . .

He looked back at Obadiah, who quickly bowed his
head, the perfect servant now, awaiting instructions. But
not quickly enough. Perhaps it had just been Ahab's
imagination, but he swore that he had seen that expression on his servant's face. The flicker, just for a moment,
of a smile.

*   *   *

The dry, cracked trail exploded with dust as the King and
his mounted bodyguards drew their horses to a halt. This
was a man in a hurry. The Septuagint version of 1 Kings
says that he 'ran out' in eagerness to meet and confront the
man who had haunted his dreams these last few years: the
most wanted man in the whole of Israel.

'So there you are, trouble-maker!' snarled Ahab, his
mouth twisted with rage. The Hebrew word for 'trou-
bler' is a very strong insult, meaning 'one who brings
disaster'.

Elijah looked back at his enemy, and decided not to
disguise the feelings of contempt that boiled within him.
He knew that this was a dangerous moment. With one
swiftly barked order, the King could have one of his
guards run the prophet through. The torture chamber
was another possibility, to encourage Elijah to reverse

the drought-curse. But God had said, 'Show yourself to the King.' Elijah spoke out:

> I have not made trouble for Israel. But you and your father's family have. You have abandoned the Lord's commands and have followed the Baals. Now summon the people from all over Israel to meet me on Mount Carmel. And bring the four hundred and fifty prophets of Baal and the four hundred prophets of Asherah, who eat at Jezebel's table (1 Kings 18:18–19).

Ahab opened his mouth to protest. After all, *he* was in charge around here, *he* gave the orders, and here was this religious fanatic upstart telling him what to do and where to go. It was outrageous! But no words came, and he was surprised to find himself just nodding meekly. The sergeant of the guard was flabbergasted. His hand sat ready on his sword, just waiting for the order to strike and silence the cursed prophet for good. But no order came and, without another word, Elijah turned and walked away.

*   *   *

It was early morning, but already the sun was high upon Carmel, giving a rippled, shimmering appearance to the crowds that were climbing the hillside. It had been like this for a few days now. It must have taken some time for the people to travel from all over Israel. By the thousand they came, many of them gaunt and thin, weakened by the drought years, struggling to the summit. They knew better than to disobey the royal decree: the King had ordered that every able-bodied person gather at Carmel, and only the fools or the dying ignored the King—with the notable exception, of course, of Queen Jezebel. She hadn't come this far by obeying or respecting her husband up until now, and she wasn't about to start. She stayed away, and her 400 Asherah priests stayed away too, by order of their royal patron. The 450 Baal priests were in attendance, and happy to be there. Carmel had become a favourite site for the evening feasts. This, they thought, was their home territory. They felt safe and secure on the mountainside.

The crowds were so thick that some fought over vantage spots. They knew that it would take hours, days even, for everyone to arrive. The rich would have taken the prime spots, jockeying to be closer to the temporary shelter which had been erected to protect the King from the scorching sun. The poor would have been unable to see a thing, probably relegated to the Kishon lowlands and kept informed by the rumours and conversations passed slowly down the hillside. Elijah was nowhere to be seen. He was most likely in one of the 2,000 caves that litter Carmel—a warrior preparing for the battle of his life.

Only when the King, his bodyguard and a huge entourage arrived did the crowd begin to talk about some action taking place. At this stage, all they knew was that the King had called them all together, and that the Gileadite Elijah was involved in the meeting as well. They waited, joked, speculated, renewed old friendships, exchanged the latest family news, showed off sons and daughters with pride. . . .

Carmel was an ideal location for the showdown between God and Baal. The mountain was always a lush green, as it was the first to catch the sea rains as the clouds marched towards the east. Of course, the Baal prophets would have been delighted by this, as Carmel would have been the one place in Israel that would show little evidence of the drought. Perhaps the people would forget the drought-judgement for a while, and consolidate their commitment to their new gods.

Carmel, however, was to be the scene of a cosmic courtroom drama, with geographical witnesses for the prosecution in the case of Yahweh versus Baal.

To the north rose the snow-capped triple peaks of Mount Hermon, the mountain itself a stark reminder to everyone, for here children had been sacrificed by fire to the Baals since the time of the Judges. A mountain that spoke of a thousand dark nights of orgies, apostasy and the murder of too many innocents.

To the west lay the clear blue waters of the Mediterranean, and the sails of Tyrian trade ships could be seen here and there—a reminder to all of the trading alliance that had been entered into with Tyre; that treaty which had caused so much trouble. Sailing ships that spoke of greed and ungodly alliances; disastrous dealing.

Then down at the foot of Carmel, beyond the Kishon River, could be seen the royal country house of Jezreel, and the huge Baal temple that stood next to it. A royal palace that housed an idolater king and a witch queen.

The witnesses gave silent testimony.

Finally came the hour when the crowds craned their necks, pointed their fingers excitedly down the hillside and muttered their speculations behind cupped hands, because the Gileadite was spotted walking steadily upwards. As he walked, he thrust the end of his staff onto the parched earth with each step—a man in the rhythm of resolve. Elijah was coming. The court was in session.

*　　*　　*

There is something eerie about the silence that can suddenly fall upon a huge crowd. One moment it is a teeming
mass, pulsating with laughter, gossip, irritation, questions,
opinions, a million mingled words. Then it seems as if
every mouth closes, every ear strains to listen, unwilling
to miss a thing—the crowd now a murmuring giant stilled.
I imagine that such a silence fell upon the huge Carmel
gathering that day so long ago, as Elijah climbed up onto a
rock, waited for the last voice to be still, and laid down the
gauntlet of challenge: 'How long will you waver between
two opinions? If the Lord is God, follow him, but if Baal
is God, follow him.'

With two sentences, Elijah brilliantly argues his case.
Point one: worshipping both God and Baal is spiritually
and intellectually debilitating. To try to do so is to waver
or, more accurately, 'limp on two crutches' or 'stagger'.
Some experts in the Hebrew language suggest that the
word used here describes a bird that is walking along a
tree branch and suddenly discovers that it splits into two.
Instead of making a choice, it puts one claw on each
branch, and tries to continue its journey, accomplishing
nothing but the splits in the process. Another translator
renders this: 'How long will you walk lame on both knee
joints?'

The whole episode reveals that Elijah possessed a sharp,
sometimes cutting and sarcastic, sense of humour. Thus
Elijah graphically demonstrates the pathetic foolishness of
religious syncretism; 'mongrel religion', as one writer
puts it. 'How long?' asks Elijah.

Point two: Elijah connects with a memory buried deep
in the hearts of the Israelites as he describes the Lord as
'Jehovah'. This was the name by which the Lord God had
been known to the people ever since their forefathers
came out from the land of Egypt. It stirred memories of

the covenant God of Abraham, Isaac and Jacob. Elijah is going for high stakes here: he wants to see a national renewal of covenant. Just as Samuel called the people to recommit themselves to Jehovah at the coronation of King Saul, so Elijah is looking for a new pledge of allegiance after 400 years of darkness and backsliding.

Point three: make your choice. Jehovah God will not foist himself upon human beings, but respects the will of a person to choose whom he will serve. It's make your mind up time. Elijah's Hebrew words most literally mean, 'If Yahweh is God, go after him; but if Baal, go after him.'

But the unearthly hush remained on the crowd. Perhaps the common people were nervous of offending the King— or unsure about the response of the Baal prophets. Whatever the reason, their silence discredited them, for they had all experienced a supernatural drought that had been initiated by a servant of Jehovah. That alone should have been enough to convince them who was really God. But doubt and rebellion are stubborn partners when they have lived too long in the human heart. It was time for the real God to stand up.

*   *   *

In human terms, it must have appeared that the odds were loaded in favour of the Baal prophets. It's good for morale to have 450 of your like-minded friends around when you're involved in an important contest—you can encourage and spur one another on as mutual cheerleaders. But Elijah stood alone. There's no record of the prophets in exile being on hand to help, and Obadiah the double agent is keeping his customary low profile. No wonder Elijah later exaggerated: 'I'm the only one of the Lord's prophets left.'

He let the Baal priests pick which bull they would use for the sacrifice—and then let them go first. But then again, none of this made the slightest bit of difference, because they were singing their songs to a dead god. It was a serenade to nothingness.

They went on for about eight solid hours. They danced until they were fit to drop—limbs aching, muscles searing with hot pain, driven on through normal thresholds of exhaustion by a frantic sense of despair. Interestingly, the Bible uses the word 'halt' or 'stagger' to describe their dancing. It is the same word that Elijah used in his 'How long will you *halt* between two opinions?' speech. Ironically, the height of the Baal frenzy included a dramatisation of the staggering that Elijah had described so powerfully earlier in the day! They shouted and screamed and sang until they were hoarse; until their feeble voices faded to a whisper: 'O Baal, hear us. . . .' The Hebrew writer of 1 Kings allows them no sense of dignity, delivering three hammer-blow phrases of indictment: 'But there was no response, no-one answered, no-one paid attention.'

For the first hour or two the crowd were probably rapt with attention. Then, like all crowds when there's no action and little hope of any developing, boredom sets in. Unrelated conversations start, the children go back to their chasing games, and the moment of tension is past.

Enter Elijah the comedian, eager to spice up the occasion with a few witty asides. One thing is sure: months and months alone with God haven't dulled his keen sense of ironic humour. In fact, while this sweaty praying is going on, Elijah is having a party. That wicked sarcasm emerges again, as he offers the exhausted idolaters some home-spun advice on how to wake a god up.

'Shout louder,' he encourages. 'Maybe he's deep in thought . . . maybe he's asleep.' This was another one of Elijah's many 'in' jokes—Baal Melqart was believed to be a vegetation deity who had to be awakened each spring from his winter hibernation;* thus the need for all the stamping and yelling. Evidently Baal needed a wake-up call.

Then the Hebrew text reveals Elijah at his earthy, out-rageous best: 'Maybe he is going to the toilet. . . .' (The translators of the NIV Bible obviously couldn't cope with such a blunt, crude character, so they've tidied the text up by having Elijah say, 'Maybe he's travelling.' Obviously Elijah wouldn't make a very good super-polite and equally bland Evangelical.) What a character! Extreme problems demand extreme solutions. View the Jesus who was good, but not 'nice', single handedly wrecking the money-changers' stalls in the Temple and you'll see what I mean.

Meanwhile, back at the sacrifice, the Baal priests fol-lowed Elijah's somewhat snide comments and indeed shouted louder. There was still no response. It was time for them to bring out their final weapon. Taking up swords and spears, they stabbed and gouged themselves until the whole area was awash with blood. Perhaps it was designed to be a hint to the apparently stupid Baal: 'Look, gods, we need fire. Bright, colourful, red stuff like this.' Or perhaps it was just another attempt at bribery. Surely Baal would have mercy on a bunch of 450 who were bleeding to death. One commentator suggests that this was a solemn act of blood bonding between worshippers and the devil

* Fensham, *A Few Observations*, p 229.

they worshipped; a bloody covenant of desperation. But it was in vain.

Eight agonising hours later, the chopped limbs of the bull-sacrifice sat, dried by the sun, but with no sign of the slightest spark. By now, the sacrifice would have been a mass of flies, eager to gorge themselves on the blood and offal, turning the Baal altar into a seething putrefying mess. This itself was testimony to the obscenity that was Baalism. But there had been no pyrotechnical response from the heavens. The truth was out. Baal was no god at all. The people had been deceived. Many of them had sacrificed their own children—and all for a lie.

The natural response from the crowd would have been one of stunned anger. Fists clenched into a knuckle-white ball, and angry words yelled that vengeance would be taken. Perhaps mothers wept as they remembered their newborn, and replayed the horrifying images of the sacrifice. In their darker moments, in the middle of hot, sleepless nights, they'd tossed and turned and tried to remember what their babies had looked like, and then, when the image of the tiny face came, they'd tried to erase it lest they be driven over the brink of madness. And in those sweating, breathless moments, they'd told themselves that the pain was worth it, because it was for the gods, a noble offering. But it was all for nothing, the slaying of their darlings for idols that couldn't hear or see; for a god that had never been. Tears of anger, recrimination, guilt and rage flowed freely.

*   *   *

And just when it may have seemed like there was no comfort—nothing that could possibly make life worth living again—the Gileadite cupped his hands to his mouth and cried: 'People! Come here to me!' No need for them to stand at a distance, for this was to be a totally genuine miracle. Let the people come as close as they liked. Truth can stand the most intense scrutiny. No second invitation was needed. The people ran to him—a great, sad, curious mass.

*   *   *

The old altar was in disarray, broken down by neglect and vandalism. Or had the destruction been the result of the Baal feasts that happened here on countless nights—a ceremonial desecration of the old Yahweh altar; another spit in the face of the living God? Carefully, Elijah picked up twelve stones, and as he wedged them together to form a new altar, he began to speak out the tribal names of Israel: 'Reuben, Simeon, Levi, Issachar, Zebulan, Dan, Naphtali, Gad, Asher, Joseph. . . . '

Then came the revolutionary revelation: the last two stones, and the accompanying words, 'Judah and Benjamin.' The crowd drew breath, and then quickly began to mutter, staggered by the prophet's act. He was suggesting that the southern kingdom, arch enemies now of Israel, should be included in one united nation under God. But before the political chattering could continue, Elijah called for a shovel, and began to dig a trench.

The true worker of miracles doesn't need to cheerlead a crowd into a frenzy of expectation. Cleverly constructed hype or crass showmanship accompanied by emotion-wrenching music isn't required in order to see the impossible. Slowly, methodically Elijah dug, pausing every now and then to wipe the sweat that beaded his brow and stained the back and armpits of his rough shirt. It was hard work, and he grunted as his body jarred each time the spade hit the hard-baked earth, but it was a necessary labour, because Elijah wanted every living soul to see that the real God needed no help, no conjuring tricks or sleight of hand. This was going to be a 100% bona-fide miracle!

Fourteen litres of water were brought from the Kishon, and they filled the trench. Elijah took some of the tinder dry wood and placed it on the altar, and then put the cut bull, carefully blooded and quartered, upon the wood. By sacrificing an ox, he made a powerful statement, and we mustn't miss the significance of it. Elijah could have called for a lamb, or a pair of doves, or a kid goat for the sacrifice. But he insisted on an ox. Why? According to the Law, whenever a priest or prophet wanted to make atonement for the sins of himself and his own immediate household only, he would offer an ox. It was a private act, rather than an offering on behalf of the people.

'Aaron is to offer the bull for his own sin offering to *make atonement for himself and his household*' (Lev 16:6, italics mine.)

So why an ox, when Elijah could have made an offering on behalf of the whole nation on Carmel? The answer is simple: quite apart from the fact that Elijah wanted to be totally clean before God himself, he had absolutely no right to make an offering on behalf of a people who had not repented for themselves. Such an offering would have been a mockery; a lifeless ceremony, void of meaning or purpose. Until the people themselves decided to engage their will and change their minds, no ceremony would have any merit. So he took an ox, because he, and he alone, wanted to be right before Yahweh. We must never forget that God refuses to overrule a person's will—be it in providing forgiveness, deliverance or whatever. As John Barr says, 'The Cross won't cover what we won't uncover.' There is a sense of sovereignty about the will of a human being.

Next, Elijah invited representatives of the people to soak the sacrifice in yet more water—a total of twelve jars full; one for each tribe. The whole altar area was a soggy mess and the ditches were thoroughly waterlogged. Impossible work—even for a man with a twentieth-century firelighter and a hundred matches!

Why the water routine? Elijah wanted the people to know that when the fire came, it really did come from God. Yahweh didn't need a hand or (unlike Baal) a hint. We do well to remember this when we are tempted to exaggerate or embellish ever-so-slightly a testimony of what God has done. There is no glory in a lie—even a well-intentioned lie. How many innocent, well-meaning people have been publicly prayed for in a healing line and, when the microphone is thrust in their face and the crowd leans forward eager to hear a good report, they feel obliged to splutter, 'Well, I feel a little better, praise God . . .'? Let a physician affirm that a true work has been done before claiming a healing. What are we afraid of? A miracle can stand the most intense scrutiny. (Of course, there are one or two investigative physicians currently appearing in the British media, claiming that they have never seen a genuine miracle. Unfortunately, one particularly outspoken doctor always explains away healings by claiming that there was an original misdiagnosis. That kind of investigation is neither impartial nor scientific.)

God isn't pleased or glorified when a leader has a 'word of knowledge' about somebody in a crowd of 500 who 'has a bad back'. Get real! Half the people there have a twinge or two in their backs, and the other half are probably wishing that they did at that moment so that they could get in on the action.

Go on, Elijah. Fill the buckets again. Splash that fire-killing water all over the place. The real God needs no help!

*   *   *

At last, all was ready. The crowd quietened, that unearthly silence again. Thousands—from the nervous, agitated Ahab resplendent in his fabulous robes to the lowliest beggars—stared at Elijah. He seemed to be waiting for something, his hands on his hips, looking at the sky, towards the sun. Some wondered if he was looking for the rays of the sun to focus on the soaked altar, but his faith wasn't in solar heat. He was just waiting for the sun to climb to that place in the sky that announced that it was, in modern terms, three o'clock in the afternoon—the time that God had decreed for the afternoon sacrifice in the Temple at Jerusalem. The people glanced frequently at the Yahweh altar. No flies spotted this sacrifice; it was kept pure, the saline sharpness of the salt repelled the insects. At last, satisfied that the moment had come, he lifted his hands and began to pray, calmly but deliberately.

*   *   *

It had been done before—by David, the friend of God. He had built an altar to God 200 years earlier, when he made the classic and oft-quoted statement, 'I will not offer to God that which costs me nothing.' God always responds to costly obedience. Fire fell from heaven and consumed David's burned offering—a swift, dynamic gesture of divine approval.

However, Elijah was inspired by more than historical precedent. This was more than a gamble: 'Well, God, I'm going to stick both your neck and mine on the block, so I sure hope that you come through.' God had spoken very specifically to Elijah—that much is revealed by a prayer which stirred up a sense of ancient destiny: 'O Lord, God of Abraham, Isaac and Israel, let it be known today that you are God in Israel and that I am your servant *and have done all these things at your command*' (1 Kings 18:36).

It was also an ideal way to strike at the evil Baal myth. For just as Baal's lordship over corn was refuted by a miracle at Zarephath, and Elijah's cutting jokes portrayed Baal as the god who needed to be yelled at in order to wake him up, so Baal was also supposed to be the god of fire. In fact, it was believed that the house where Baal lived was made and tested by fire. Time for another one of those ancient inscriptions written thousands of years ago about Baal and the house that a personality called Kothat-wa-Hasis was supposed to have built for him. It helpfully throws light on this idea:

Fire is set on the house, flame on the palace,
Behold a day and a second, fire eats into the house
Flame into the palace, a third, a fourth day,
Fire eats into the house, flame into the palace.
A fifth, a sixth day, fire eats into the house.
Flame, in the midst of the palace, Behold on the seventh day,
The fire departs from the house, the flame from the palace.
Silver turns from blocks, gold is turned from bricks.

The popular myth was that Baal was literally at home with fire. But the flames were not destined to come from that non-existent palace furnace in the sky, but from the hand of the true God, Yahweh.

Was there a moment when nothing happened? A few seconds that would have felt like minutes to the crowd, now on tiptoe? We'll never know, but we do know that Elijah continued to speak to God. It was a brief, succinct prayer—no time spent rambling around in word circles, trying to stir faith; no 'vain repetitions' here. 'Answer me, O Lord, answer me, so these people will know that you, O Lord, are God, *and that you are turning their hearts back again*' (1 Kings 18:37, italics mine).

Delay or not, the final words of the prophet's prayer were significant and provided the trigger for the power of God. It was when Elijah stated the need for the nation to repent and turn back to God that the miracle was ignited. No wonder he was the forerunner of John the Baptist. God has no interest in providing cosmic firework displays for the sake of thrilling interested spectators. Signs and wonders are purposeful, designed to elicit response from rebellious human hearts.

*   *   *

It all took just five stunning seconds, but it would be the focus of countless conversations around evening camp fires for hundreds of years. The little children who, at the moment of impact and ignition, had been snatched and clutched close by fearful mothers, would remember the terrible fire for the rest of their lives, and would thrill

their own grandchildren as they recalled the event. The
day that they saw the hand of God.

It was shocking in its suddenness, and in its awesome
power. It came from no cloud, for in drought-stricken
Israel the sun rode high and unchallenged in a clear blue
sky. This was not lightning. It was not a spontaneous
ignition from within; some cleverly provoked combus-
tion, for they saw the fire flash from the heavens, blinding
white hot as it seared through the still afternoon air and
smothered the altar in a second, evaporating the water and
leaving only hissing, sizzling charcoal where the wood
and the bull had been just a moment before.

Perhaps the crowd stood impossibly still and quiet for
ten or fifteen seconds, their minds struggling to catch up
with what their eyes had just witnessed. And then one
solitary voice began to cry out, choking with tears, 'The
Lord, he is God! The Lord, he is God!' And then a nation
fell on its face, and it pushed itself as low as it could into
the baked earth. The solo became the anthem of thousands, as in unison Israel made the spontaneous declara-
tion of truth—a great roar of what appeared to be genuine
repentance and faith: 'The Lord, he is God! The Lord, he
is God!'

Sharp commentators have observed that their cry did
not include a personal pronoun: 'The Lord, he is *our* God,
or *my* God. . . . . ' Perhaps Elijah would recall that lack of
personal commitment later. Who knows what Ahab did in
those historic moments? Did he remain solidly on his
throne, an angry sneer smearing his face? Or did he do
the politically expedient thing, and join in with the shouting? We can be sure that among the thousands, there were
450 who refused to join in—a silent, unyielding protest.
The prophets of Baal had no song to sing, no cheer to
offer. And after a while, as inevitably the cries of worship

subsided and the people slowly began to climb to their feet, all eyes were turned on the men who had led a whole nation into deception. They had shattered families and brought about the drought-judgement because of their despicable wickedness. The verdict was clear: the prophets of Baal were guilty. Time for justice and, according to the Law that had been ignored for so long, only one sentence could be passed on an idolater. It was time for death.

*   *   *

The people were quick to obey when Elijah ordered the arrest of the bruised and bleeding Baal prophets. Some of them were probably nearly dead already from the loss of blood they suffered from self-inflicted wounds. Ignoring their cries and demonic curses, they dragged them all, arms pinioned, down through the thick Carmel undergrowth, to the Valley of Kishon. By the low waters of the river, where Judge Barak had triumphed over the Syrians years earlier, they ran them through with the sword, good victorious over evil again, a fitting place. It was no lynch mob, but a just execution.

In the lengthening shadows of the late afternoon, the swords flashed again and again. This was God's judgement for the babies who would never grow up—little lives snuffed out by the fire; for the mothers who would be crippled by guilt and grief until their dying day; for the young men and women who had lost their innocence for ever, recruited to serve as temple prostitutes, condemned to lurk in the 'sacred' groves for years, ready to embrace the next sweating stranger. The condemned most likely died as they had lived: crying out to gods Melqart and Asherah, even then refusing to believe that they had sold their lives for an empty lie. The Kishon River reddened, flowing back as it did towards Phoenicia—bad blood going home, and good riddance. A mass grave was probably hastily dug, and the bodies thrown in without ceremony. The place became known as Tell-el-Kass: the priests' mound.

*   *   *

It had been a full day—the fullest day of Elijah's life. He had battled with Gargantuan pressures, and overthrown the forces of darkness. He had been taxed to the very limit of his psychological resources. He must have been exhausted—and if ever a man could have been tempted to say, 'Enough is enough. I've done my part,' it was Elijah. He could have been forgiven, perhaps, for wanting to linger on the lower slopes to shake 10,000 hands and receive as many words of warm congratulations, for he was a hero now.

However, the work wasn't finished yet. Elijah walked up to the very summit of Carmel, conscious that the sky was still a flaming, shimmering sheet of brass. As ever, it's time to pray again. A boy or young man joined him, simply described in Scripture as 'his servant'. We can't be sure about the identity of this person. Legend has it that he may have been the widow's son from Zarephath, dedicated to serve the man whom God had used to deliver him from death. He may have been a volunteer from the crowd, eager to bless the man who asked God for fire.

He may have been Elisha in the first faltering steps of ministry.

As they climbed, the powder dry dust clouded around their heels, their leather sandals slapping the brittle, unyielding earth. But Elijah climbed with a promise from God in his heart: 'Go and show yourself to Ahab . . . and I will send rain.' He had the promise, but he still had to possess the promise, for God was working in partnership with this man. I wonder how many times we frustrate God because we read and believe in the promises of Scripture, but we refuse to fulfil God's conditions (for many of the promises of God come with clear conditions), or wrestle in prayer in order to lay hold of those blessings.

The lessons that Elijah had learned in the lonely years paid off now, because even though earlier in the day fire had jumped out of the sky the first time he asked for it, now he had to send his servant out seven times before receiving the weather report he wanted to hear. I won't labour the point by making obscure statements about the vague typological significance of the number seven. Suffice it to say that Elijah didn't give up, but, to use an old term, 'he prayed through'. And in his perseverance, he was gifted with an ability to sense, feel and hear what others could never perceive. 'I hear the roar of rain approaching.' But there was no audible sound to be heard. There were no clouds in the sky, and the sea remained a dazzling mirror, reflecting the deep blue of a cloudless sky. But Elijah heard something from God, and so the negative weather forecast didn't worry him at all.

At last, the servant reported a cloud-sighting. It was no bigger than a man's hand, mind, but it was enough for Elijah. He jumped up, a man utterly alive and bouncing with an exuberant, extravagant joy. He told his servant to rush down and tell the King to get himself home quickly, for the floods were coming. (Once again, the prophet telling the King what to do and when!) It was a sound piece of advice, for the ground had been hard baked for over three years. Water that would normally seep down into thirsty sub-soil would initially be unable to break through the concrete-like crust. Flash floods were inevitable.

*   *   *

It was a troubled, confused Ahab who ordered his charioteers to head for home with speed. As the fine Arabians were urged on faster by the whips and screams of the horsemen, he pondered the fact that life had been turned upside down. Why was it that Elijah seemed to be calling the shots at every opportunity, telling him where to meet, and now when to eat? Who was King around here? And then, a hideous, seeping fear that threatened to overwhelm his mind totally was beginning to take dark shape. He had been visibly shaken when the fire came. Could it *really* be that Yahweh was truly God after all? If that was the case, then where did that leave him, a King who had mocked Yahweh and led a nation after Baal?

Perhaps he then thought about the executions of the Baal prophets. He was no stranger to blood. He'd laughed when Jezebel had sported by torturing some of Yahweh's servants, and hadn't even flinched when finally they had been beheaded in the palace courtyard, a gory entertainment for the day's end. It wasn't the wholesale slaughter that disturbed him—it was more the reaction that he anticipated would explode at home when his bride discovered what had happened. Again, he must have wondered who exactly was in charge. His wife? The Tishbite? Yahweh?

And then he heard the cry of his horseman, and followed his pointed finger.

Incredibly, it was Elijah, his camel skin cloak tucked up into his belt, running at such a great speed that Ahab blinked twice in order to assure himself that, on this strangest of days, he was not hallucinating. It was no mirage. In fact, the glaring sun that had turned the land into a blast furnace for those last three years seemed to have died suddenly. It was as if a black storm was chasing behind Elijah as he came striding up towards the rattling, bumping royal chariot. And then, impossibly, the grinning prophet overtook the King—his strong, bronzed legs working like pistons, his breath punctuating the air in great, measured gasps. His laughing eyes seemed ablaze with a power that sent a shudder down Ahab's spine. Off into the distance he sped, the King following. Biblical normality was momentarily restored to Israel: the King was following the prophet.*

There have been some commentators who have suggested that Elijah was out of the will of God by going back to Jezreel, and that his leaping like a gazelle past the King was a tacky display of pride. It was a work of the flesh that Elijah dashed back to civilisation in order to be able to bask in the spotlight of success and affirmation. To argue their case, they point to the fact that no direct instruction from God specifically ordering Elijah back to Jezreel is recorded in Scripture. This is seen to be conclusive proof that Elijah was out of line, and consumed

---

*Robert L. Cohn, *Literary Logic of 1 Kings 17–19* (JBL, 1982), p 341.

with a pride that contributed to the fall that was shortly to come.

I totally disagree with these negative analyses. Elijah had just come from the place of fervent prayer, and this was the kind of praying that brings three-year droughts to an instant, waterlogged conclusion. It should also be noted that Elijah's running ability was nothing short of supernatural, probably unrivalled even in Olympic circles today. Why was he able to cruise past the King's finest Arabians with ease? Scripture provides the answer: 'The hand of the Lord was upon him.' This is a term that denotes favour and blessing.

No, Elijah went back to Jezreel under divine steam— and how very logical it was that he did so. The man had just presided over a gathering which had climaxed in a national cry of repentance, or so it seemed. Now he would need to be on hand, close to the corridors of power, in order to respond strategically to the unfolding events to come.

*   *   *

As the figure of Elijah became a dot in the distance and finally disappeared over a hill, it was as if the clouds exploded and great trapdoors suddenly sprang open releasing millions of gallons in a few moments, causing the ground itself to sizzle in shock. The drought was over. Ahab stared wildly into the rain, and longed for the familiar safety of home . . . and his wife.

6

Prophet at a Loss

Those who believe they believe in God, but without passion in the heart, without anguish of mind, without uncertainty, without doubt, and even at times without despair, believe only in the idea of God, and not in God Himself (Madeleine L'Engle).

Now Ahab told Jezebel everything Elijah had done and how he had killed all the prophets with the sword. So Jezebel sent a messenger to Elijah to say, 'May the gods deal with me, be it ever so severely, if by this time tomorrow I do not make your life like that of one of them' (1 Kings 19:1).

It was most likely that Elijah returned to a virtually deserted Jezreel. No crowds would have turned out to meet the new hero, because most were still struggling back through the waterlogged roads from Carmel—a journey that would take at least a couple of days. Even the King was still en route. Jezreel would have been a veritable ghost town. Only the old people, too infirm to travel for the Carmel contest, plus those disinterested enough to ignore the royal decree, would have remained in the city. And then, of course, there were those who were so committed to Baal that they remained behind, hoping that the fact that the Queen, her entourage and the prophets of Ashteroth had declined to appear would provide them with a political insurance policy.

Elijah would have found a place of lodging, and then waited. It would not be long. Within twenty-four hours the common people, exhausted from their journey, splattered and caked with mud, would have trailed their last few weary steps through the city gates, a glad smile on their faces. It was good to be home. The King himself was back in the city too. It was noted that he had not paused a moment to return the greetings and bows of his subjects as he sped into the city. He had quickly disappeared into the whitewashed walls of the palace.

As Jezreel once again became a throbbing, thriving metropolis, Elijah probably became something of a celebrity. It would have become difficult for him to go out of his lodgings, with people wanting to talk to him everywhere he went—conversations that would have taken all day and all night. As he walked through the city, fingers were probably pointed at him; children rushed up and grabbed his camel skin, eager to be around the famous man. How totally alive he felt, as if electricity was flowing through every nerve in his body. His mind was racing, packed full of ideas. The people had rejected the Baals, and now further action would need to be taken.

He pondered the events to come, imagining with relish the wonder of Israel walking hand in hand with the true God once again. There would be a summons to the palace. The King would be eager to consult with the prophet of Yahweh. A season of repentance and fasting would be ordered by royal decree. Units of the army would be sent up and down the nation to seek out and destroy the Baal altars and bring any resident Baal prophets to justice. The Ashteroth prophets would have to be dealt with. Legislation would be handed down from the King to prevent the curse of Baalism ever rising again in Israel. Perhaps there would be a public reading of the Law, and a rededication of all of the male children who had been dedicated by circumcision to Baal.

It was all too wonderful, a dream come true, but repeatedly Elijah allowed his imagination to go wild as he considered the bright and glorious days ahead. God was continuing to kiss the ground with rain, millions of beautiful gallons, the smile of Yahweh spread broadly over Israel again.

One nagging, lurking thought remained. Jezebel. Born and raised in the service of Baal. Murderess of the prophets, exterminator of the schools. Would she, too, turn?

*   *   *

Deep in the heart of the palace, in the Queen's bed chamber, sat Jezebel. Her beautiful face was a twisted, snarling mask of ugly rage, her fists clenched until her knuckles stood out white as she marched up and down the fabulous room. She had tried to control herself when her snivelling pathetic little husband had told her all that Elijah had done. She noticed that he had carefully avoided all mention of Yahweh, knowing that the mention of that name was not good for peace. Instead he had centred on the actions of the prophet from Gilead. When she heard about his mocking of the Baal priests, she became quietly enraged. She struggled to maintain her composure, locking her facial muscles into a look of quiet interest as her husband spoke. But when she heard about the Kishon massacre, she felt her head swimming with a blind, insane hatred. Unable to contain herself any longer, she made her excuses and rushed out of the throne room to the safety of her private chambers.

Now, one solitary thought dominated all others: the desire for vengeance. She would get even, and in doing so, she would wipe the memory of this fire-breathing prophet from Israel for ever. With a scream that demanded instant attention or else, she summoned her servants.

*   *   *

Perhaps he was sleeping when it happened—dreaming of drought, fire and death. Perhaps in his vivid nightmare the lifeless eyes of 450 stared accusingly at him, their bodies suddenly coming to life again—the broken, bloodied Baal priests rising again, a satanic resurrection, rising again to march back in triumph to Jezreel. . . .

Suddenly, the royal messenger was framed in the doorway, his chest heaving from the run, a hint of mockery in his eyes. Elijah wearily shook his head as if to shake off fatigue in a moment, and wiped the sleep from his eyes.

Elijah carefully searched his face for a hint of the words to come. Obviously enjoying his brief moment of power, the messenger took his time. Patiently the prophet waited.

'You've gone too far this time, old man. I've seen Her Majesty in a temper before, but never like this. Never.' The envoy paused, and remembered, and then the arrogance was gone, his eyes clouded with fear as he recalled the scene back at the palace. 'When the King told her about Carmel, and about how you killed her prophets, she flew into such a rage, I swear that her personal attendants were all beside themselves with terror. And then she went quiet for a long time. I'm not sure which was worse: the screaming or the silence.'

Tiredness seemed suddenly to overwhelm Elijah's body, and with it came a growing, gnawing sense of fear about what was to come. He didn't have to wait long. The royal envoy continued.

'The Queen called her friends together, and said that she had a very important vow to swear, and that everybody was to attend her to witness it. She screamed out the names of her gods at the top of her voice, ran her finger across her throat, and carefully pronounced the self-curse. She told me to repeat it to you very carefully, Elijah. Word for word.'

Straightening himself up as if to deliver a formal sentence, the messenger continued: 'May the gods deal with me, be it ever so severely, if by this time tomorrow, Elijah, I do not make your life like that of one of them.'

Suddenly the messenger was gone, the echo of his words ringing in the chamber. What was it she had said? 'If I do not make your life like one of them. . . .'

The imagery was chilling, as he remembered the killing field called Kishon. Bloodied bodies piled high, corpse upon corpse, eyes staring, a hill of death. 'Like one of them. . . .'

Suddenly, uncontrollably, he began to shake.

*   *   *

Why did the Queen send a messenger to Elijah with an announcement of his forthcoming death? After all, she could have just sent an assassin along to get the job done immediately. She had put all the other prophets to death, so why not just despatch Elijah? To warn him was to take the risk that he would run (as indeed he did). So why the registered letter containing a death threat?

It's possible that she sent a letter rather than a hired hit-man because she knew that, despite her great power, she would be going too far if she actually killed Elijah. I doubt if she feared her husband. She had him pretty well eating out of the palm of her hand. Perhaps, for the first time, she feared the common people. If they could turn on the prophets of Baal, they could storm the palace as well if she murdered their hero.

Or did Jezebel opt for the messenger because she had discovered a satanic secret weapon? Certainly it would take a special attack to bring this hitherto invincible man down. He had stood before the highest authority in the land and denounced him. He had challenged 400 witches, knowing the dark power that was theirs, a gift from devils rather than gods. It was time to use the weapon that she had triumphed with repeatedly down through her dark years.

Fear. A threat or a suggestion of terrors to come is often more intimidating than the action itself. She would manipulate the man from Gilead with words—clutch hold of his soul and hang on with a vice-like grip, and cause him to destroy himself. And what a master she was in the evil art of manipulation. The Septuagint version includes Jezebel adding to the message: 'As sure as I am Jezebel, and you are Elijah.' Think about that. Very carefully chosen words, proclaiming her royalty, power and importance ('I am Jezebel') and her enemy's nothing-ness, in human terms—a mere peasant from the hills ('You are Elijah'). She was ripping his sense of God-given identity right out of his soul. It was a brilliant tactic—inspiration from hell itself. And it worked.

Sudden transformation. Black turned to white. Raging furnace fire turned to blistering white ice. Colourful life turned to cold death. Vibrant faith turned to desolate doubt where there is nothing left to live for.

In a few seconds, this awful metamorphosis churned inside Elijah's heart and mind with such a force that he seemed to become a different man altogether. The ballistic missile called fear vaporised in a second the memory of all that God had done for and through Elijah. He became like a staggering insomniac, shocked into forgetting everything he had so painstakingly learned.

Wiped away, like a duster wipes chalk from a chalkboard. His prophecy about the drought. Raven waiters. Flour and oil shall not be spent . . . and then resurrection for a sick boy in Zarephath. Firebolts from the shimmering blue sky. Drought-shattering downpours because he said so. Bionic marathon running that put the royal charioteers to shame. All part of history, all very real, but the reality shattered by a venomous dart called fear.

Then the man who had stood strong in his God on Carmel tumbled down into a spiritual and psychological pit—bottomless and dark. A place where hope, laughter, vision and God himself are all dead.

He should have stood his ground. Like a long-distance runner who completes twenty-six miles and then stops ten feet from the elusive finishing tape, he was a winner almost to the end—and then he snapped. He should have taken the attitude of the ancient character Chrysostom, who was also sent a threatening letter by the Empress Eudoxia, and his reply was, 'Go tell her I fear nothing but sin.'

Yet he didn't do the right thing, the heroic thing. Fuelled by a mad, illogical panic, he ran. And how he ran! Elijah staggered in a blind fog for a day's journey, desperate for safety, only to then turn around and pray for death. But this was no short-lived thing; a brief overnight stay in the smothering hold of depression. It was far more serious than that. His faithful servant was sent away, and he embarked on a lengthy trek through the wilderness. The journey should not have taken him anywhere near that long, unless he got hopelessly lost.

What went through his tortured mind during those long searing furnace days, and those crushing, lonely nights when he lay under the stars hearing only the plaintive wailing of jackals? Did he wonder about the Hebrews, who had tramped these sands for forty long years so long ago? Where was the pillar of cloud that had greeted their waking? Where was the blazing pillar of fire that had lit up their dark nights? Deep, hopeless despair etched into his face as he wearily continued, a man in mourning, grieving the death of his soul, and of his God.

Freeze the frame for a moment. Stop with me and see an amazing, pitiful sight: the hero of Carmel now a suicidal fugitive; the prophet who rebuked a diabolical dictator King now scurrying away like a frightened rat scared by a flashlight. The question has to be asked: Why? What were the fatal flaws that caused this cataclysmic collapse?

How are the mighty fallen: disappointment with God

When great hopes and dreams are shattered in a moment, depression quickly settles in on the human soul. The bride who prepares for months for her wedding, only to stand in the entrance of a crowded church and be told that the man whom she thought was hers is not planning to attend the ceremony—ever—is someone who knows the excruciating emptiness of joy murdered by despair. The woman who delivers her child after nine long wearisome months;

whose eyes brighten with the thrill and anticipation of seeing her son or daughter for the first time, only to be told that her love is still-born—she knows the ecstasy and then the agony.

Elijah knew that kind of pain. He had breathed the air of hope deep into his soul—had felt that a new day had dawned after hundreds of years of blackest night—only to be told that the revival was hereby cancelled, by royal decree. There would be no turning, no revolution: the disgusting status quo was to continue. Nothing could ever reach the heart of Jezebel—that dung-woman. He'd followed God's instructions to the letter—and it was all one great terrible, exhausting failure.

Ever felt like that? The chances are that if you have, you kept the thoughts and feelings which nagged away at you very carefully hidden. The truth is, there are times when God seems to let us down. We pray. And pray. We try to stir our hearts to faith, and hope for a miracle begins to form. We begin to be confident that God is going to work just as we have asked him to; that he will respond to operate according to our plan—'Plan A' we'll call it.

There are times, however, when Plan A doesn't ever materialise. To put it bluntly, God has a habit of being God, and acting like God, and that means there are times when he has another plan—Plan B, if you like. Elijah was a Plan A man. He had read and rehearsed and prayed and fasted through Plan A until he knew it backwards: Ahab and Jezebel would lead the nation in repentance, and so on.

God, however, had another plan, and Ahab and Jezebel had no part in it. He was writing them out of the script altogether. Jezebel particularly was beyond redemption. She had a callous heart that had been unmoved as the little children begged for mercy before the sacrificial knife. No firebolt from heaven was ever going to get her attention, and God knew that. He had other plans that were far more radical and revolutionary than Elijah could have imagined, and the wretched, pathetic royal family had been given their last chance already. Now they were written out of the screenplay for good as far as God was concerned. As we will see later, the Lord had another man waiting in the wings—a man prepared and anointed and ready to reign.

However, like you and me, Elijah hadn't read the script. (I'm glad that God keeps a lot of the future hidden from us too. There may well be some things out on the horizon that I'd rather be totally ignorant of right now.) Now of course, God could have told Elijah some of Plan B—enough to help him to stand firm during this emotional hurricane, if he had just waited long enough to listen. But fear is deafening. It screams in our ears and drowns out even God's voice. A day or two of quiet trust would have enabled Elijah to tune out the distortion and interference that screamed in his ears, and enabled him to realise that Jezebel's threat was little more than idle chatter. (Later, when Elijah appeared in public again and she had opportunity to fulfil her threat, she never did so.) But he didn't stop long enough to hear the real voice of authority, and so confusion and fear took control.

I know there are times in life when two plus two seems to equal five. Times when all the wonderful truths that we believe seem to turn to dust, or writing on yellowing canvas that stands only to mock us rather than comfort us. And the temptation is to run from God; to flee. No amount of clever little sayings or clichés will keep you anchored. You may not understand now—and you may never understand in your lifetime. But it's trust—that quiet but desperate handhold—which causes you to cry

out with Job, 'Though he slay me, yet will I bless him.'
Trust will keep your feet anchored. But Elijah forgot that,
and waved goodbye to God—and friendship too.

How are the mighty fallen: terminal loneliness

The long months spent at Zarephath had been designed to
teach Elijah the value of warm human relationships. The
isolation and exile of Cherith were only a temporary
phase. But now, as he reached the limits of his strength,
just when he needed the comfort and encouragement that
true friendship brings, Elijah dismissed his servant. Some
commentators have applauded this as a noble act, that the
prophet sent his unnamed friend back to civilisation
because he wanted to spare him a tiresome hike through
the inhospitable desert with a prophet (retired) who would
have been quite hopeless at conversation! But as Elijah
left his servant at Beersheba, which was very likely a city
of refuge, he gets no round of applause from me. I believe
that he rejected a vital resource when he launched out
stubbornly on his own—and the word that God spoke to
him later, encouraging him that there were actually 7,000
faithful left in Israel, and instructing him to anoint Elisha
as prophet to join him, seems to confirm my suspicion.
Elijah desperately needed friends. He tried to carry a
Gargantuan load upon his shoulders single-handedly—
and like a champion weightlifter, who manages for a
while to hold up an impossible burden, his arms shaking
with strain, blood vessels and veins popping out on his
blood-filled face, he suddenly snapped. The champion of
Carmel collapsed.

Nothing has changed. I am constantly meeting Christians who are dying of terminal loneliness—and some of
the worst cases of this ancient and modern disease are to

be found among leaders. Too many times in recent weeks I have sat in homes and restaurants with Christian leaders, some successful (whatever that means), others struggling, but all who smile brightly in public, talk eloquently about love and the blessings of fellowship and who have broken down and wept like babies when asked who their friends are.

In some cases the fault lies with education and training. Many young Bible college students preparing for the traditional clergy model of ministry are taught that it is inappropriate to have friendship with people who are part of the congregation they lead, lest others consider that they are favouring one member of the church over another. What utter rubbish! The church is a family, not a corporation. Why should leaders be motivated and dominated by the immature jealousy of others? Envy needs to be repented of, not pandered to.

Jesus modelled a relational leadership among a group of disciples who were highly prone to pettiness and jealousy. It was his hand-picked twelve who argued about who would get the best seats and who would get the cheap seats in the kingdom of heaven. It was the twelve who wanted to call down fire from heaven and nuke anybody who did signs and wonders who were not part of their outfit. They wanted to franchise the kingdom.

But in an atmosphere where he could have so easily been misunderstood and criticised, Jesus had his own small group of particularly close friendships. That group was a triumvirate: Peter, James and John. They had front row seats for the transfiguration. Only they were allowed in when Jesus raised Peter's mother-in-law—the others were left to stand outside (probably complaining about the injustice of their being excluded).

And it was the famous three who were invited to go

forward with Jesus in Gethsemane and watch with him as he knelt in his own open-air condemned cell; special friends for death row. Of the three, John seems singled out as the one closest to him—'the disciple whom Jesus loved'.

How many leaders are there around the world right now who are expected to preach like Spurgeon, have the wisdom of Solomon, nurture *Waltons/Little House on the Prairie* lookalike families, pray twenty-four hours a day, and yet have no one to share their fears, doubts and sins with? Those who have taught such isolation have nurtured a generation of shadowland human beings who can never be real and honest about themselves long enough to enjoy walking in the light. A spurious education indeed.

Of course there are many other Christians, in both leadership and non-leadership roles, who are lonely simply because they don't have *time* for relationships— they're too busy attending services or meetings. Not only is the diary packed full of events, but all too often those events contain no opportunity for friendship. Learning and singing have in some churches totally replaced relationship. The idea is that Bible study and prayer are *really* spiritual. Evangelism and giving are way up there on the holy list too, but laughter, sharing and friendship are demoted to being helpful but not really grade A spirituality. So we do all that stuff over a cup of tea after the service. As one pastor friend said to his congregation in my hearing, 'Now I know this isn't very spiritual, but we have a golf tournament next week.' Who said it isn't spiritual? Why should we carve our lives up into little segments, causing us to live in a bizarre schizophrenia?

We need to find ways of making time for one another in our public gatherings. At least as much time should be spent in small group activity as in larger style celebrations

and worship times. We need to abandon a 'service' men-
tality. There are no such things as services in the New
Testament church—only meetings. Ask Paul or Barnabas
if he enjoyed the service and you would be greeted by an
expression of utter bewilderment. The early church *met*:
they met God, met one another, shared and celebrated and
ate and drank and listened to preaching until way past
midnight! Down with services—long live meetings!

The church really is a family, and that means more than
exchanging a quick hand-shake or hug for forty-five seconds during the service, or singing 'Bind us together'
9,000 times before we go home. The church is more
than a Sunday feeding trough where scattered numbers
of individuals come together, sit in their plush lined
feeding stall and have a snack of worship and word to
get them through another week of individualistic, private
living. It is a community of Christ together—a genuine
family in every sense, related by shed blood.

Elijah knew none of this, so he dismissed his servant,
and did what so many of us modern believers do when we
go through trial and difficulty. Instead of crying out for
help and standing our ground, we run for our lives, only to
find that even when we get somewhere else, nothing has
changed, for we have taken ourselves, our attitudes, our
problems and our sins along with us for the ride. So Elijah
runs for his life—and then prays for death. The scenery
was very different. He was in an area which was beyond
the rule of Ahab, so technically he was safe. But within
him still beat a heart paralysed by fear—and he couldn't
run from that.

How are the mighty fallen: losing a sense of perspective

Elijah ran into a wilderness of despair because he saw death in Jezebel's message—and he saw the end of his own calling and ministry as well. He saw this opposition as especially significant and devastatingly meaningful. It was all over simply because he received a note. And the man who had forgotten so much about God in a few fear-filled seconds finally broke down and forgot who he himself was. No longer was he the chosen of Yahweh, the fearless anointed. He was raped of identity by his own terror, and he complained that he was no better than his ancestors (who, by the way, aren't even named in the Bible). He threw everything away in response to one demonic action instigated with brilliant cunning by Jezebel.

I can identify with Elijah: there have been too many times when I have felt like giving up my calling to ministry because of one single isolated incident which made me say, 'That's it! It's all over,' or, with Elijah, I've yelled at God and anyone else who might happen to be listening, *'I have had enough!'* How grateful I am that God gave me a wife who can help me gain perspective when I am tempted to overreact.

When I was a pastor, I remember storming into our house one dark Monday morning. After a difficult week-end, someone had made what I felt to be an unkind remark at the office, and it was to me the proverbial straw that broke the camel's back. My wife Kay was ironing as I rushed in, and I yelled at the top of my voice, 'That's *it!* I am resigning.'

She carried on ironing. I was irritated beyond belief. Here was I, limping pathetically in the shadow of death, and she had nothing to say.

I repeated the statement again, with increased decibels. Silence.

For the third time I repeated my statement of defeat, by now desperate for a reaction. I got one. Without looking up from her ironing, Kay said, 'You don't even know how to spell resignation.' I couldn't help it, I had to laugh, and in a few minutes was incredulous that I should read so much significance into one earlier comment.

We do tend to sacramentalise life though. For many Christians everything has to have a meaning. Every happening must carry some message from God, a lesson to be learned. It begins with the new convert driving down the street and praying somewhat fearfully that he will go to the mission field if the next light is green (meaning, 'The Lord says, "Go!"'). Sounds crazy? Let me tell you that I have frequently mentioned this practice in various churches around the world and you'd be amazed at how many Christians somewhat sheepishly put their hands up to admit to having tried this practice. I did it myself, only I cheated. I saw the light in the distance, and it was indeed green. In a blind panic, I jammed the brakes on immediately, and slowed a whole line of traffic down to snail-pace, until finally the light turned red—and my obligation to serve God in mosquito-infested far-flung shores was relieved.

Or there are the Christians who catch a cold or run out of petrol and wonder what God is trying to teach them. I have a revelation for them: 'Wear a balaclava and stop at petrol stations more frequently,' says the Lord. . . .

While God can and will undeniably teach us things as we walk through the different circumstances of life, we should be wary of trying to read a word from God into everything that happens. Elijah got a letter from Jezebel—and he acted as if he had received a letter from God.

How are the mighty fallen: holding a private pity party

Elijah had been called to do all kinds of very difficult things in his life, but never once do we hear him complain—until now. And how he complains! It's as if a great plaintive wail rises from his heart, as a paralysing self-pity that locks his mind and freezes his heart possesses him. Over breakfast, God asks him, 'What are you doing here?' Check out his speech of response: 'I have been very zealous for the Lord God Almighty. The Israelites have rejected your covenant, broken down your altars, and put your prophets to death with the sword. I am the only one left, and now they are trying to kill me too' (1 Kings 19:10).

Twice Elijah repeats his little speech word for word in the hearing of God. His mind is locked solidly on a single track which he seems unable to break out of. One has to concede that at least he is being honest about his feelings.

However, he is only partly right: self-pity has a way of distorting our perception of what is really the true situation. Let us put the speech under the microscope:

'I have been very zealous.' (We'll give you that one, Elijah. You really have done rather well up to now. But just one little point: why are you saying it in your whiny, complaining tone of voice? Doesn't God know that you've been zealous? Do you regret the level of commitment that you've offered to him?)

'The Israelites have rejected your covenant, broken down your altars. . . . ' (Yes, they have, but what about Carmel? The altar was rebuilt there. Yes, Jezebel is as stubborn as ever, but does that mean that the whole nation is going to follow in her wicked footsteps?)

'. . . and put your prophets to death with the sword.'

(Actually, it was that nasty lady who did that . . . remember?)

'I am the only one left.' (No, no! There are actually still 7,000 faithful in Israel. You're not on your own at all, Elijah. You just feel that way because you dismissed your servant and popped off on a vacation to self-imposed solitary confinement.)

'And now they are trying to kill me too.' (Jezebel is, Elijah; not 'they'. You remind me of the lady who told me once that everybody was leaving the church. I instantly visualised crowds streaming out of the door. Actually, 'everybody' meant that she alone was planning on leaving the church.)

Self-pity blurs our ability to see clearly. Never make a significant decision about life when you are meandering around in the fog of self-pity. It may feel rather good to go the 'nobody loves me, everybody hates me, let's snack on worms' route, but such decision-making will inevitably lead to disaster.

How are the mighty fallen: ignoring the physical

Elijah forgets God, self—and common sense. So dark is his despair that he neglects even the basic necessities of life, like food and drink. His only prayer is for a sleep from which he will never wake up. So an angel is hastily despatched to cook for the worn out and by now malnourished man of God. Notice that the angel touches him (twice in fact), but this is not a miraculous touch that spiritually turbo-charges him—rather, it's a wake-up call from God; a nudge from the heavenlies to announce that breakfast is cooked and waiting to be eaten. This was an act of great tenderness. No angels appeared to Elijah during his heady days on Carmel; no supernatural being cooked a celebratory supper when the sickly child was raised back in Zarephath; but now the man who thinks that the dried bones of his grandparents are worth more than he is gets to meet one of God's supernatural warriors.

Yet this was more than tender care: this was a deeply practical act. Elijah certainly needed the power of the Holy Spirit to flood his life afresh, but he also needed a couple of good wholesome meals in his stomach, for 'the journey was too great for him'. Not all of his depression was due to fear or 'the attack of the enemy', to coin the phrase that Christians are so fond of. Some of his depression was rooted in the fact that he had been overtaxing himself and obviously not taking care of his body.

Sometimes we Christians seem to forget that we have bodies too. We begin to feel somewhat emotionally drained, and instead of making sure that we are eating a balanced diet, getting enough sleep and recreation, and seeing to other practical issues, we are prone to announcing that the devil is on our case and we ask for prayer, as it appears there are 27,000 demons camping in our bathroom. I have been guilty of this type of ignorance in my own counselling ministry. When I was a pastor, we had a wonderful group of ladies in the church who were really keen for God, but who occasionally became emotionally low and would ask for prayer and counsel. I would pray and rebuke every available demonic principality that I could think of, until one day I realised that these 'satanic attacks' were occurring, on average, about once every twenty-eight days . . . (thankfully this rhythm of life did not hit every female in the church at the same time in each month!).

Sometimes I make mention of this in public meetings in churches, whereupon eyebrows go into orbit because it seems that this speaker is talking about 'that'. . . .

Be sensible! Why have a punch-up with the devil when an early night and a healthy meal would do the trick?

*   *   *

Days of raging sunshine snapping and licking at his neck, searching for flesh. Three hundred weary miles through the searing Sinai peninsula. Like a blind man lost, he struggled, desperately trying to suppress the death wish. This was a stubborn despair. Even a visit from an angel disguised as a fast food cook didn't shift the jet-black cloud in his heart. Onward he stumbled through the sand all day, stopping in the afternoon heat to rest. At night he slept with tears damp on his face, his mind frantically fighting off vivid visions of armies of demons, all of them pointing at him, the ex-champion. Every night the dream was the same. They just stood there, lines of them: black, impish accusers. And they said nothing. They just pointed gnarled fingers at him . . . and laughed.

7

The Steadfast Lover

Beersheba had been a haven in more ways than one. The land there was lush and fertile; a broad, inviting valley. As Elijah headed due south towards Mount Haleiqim, and the landscape became barren, bleak and treeless, it seemed that the changing scenery more accurately reflected the state of his heart. Scattered rocks strewn around only momentarily irritated him by day, but as dusk slowly extinguished the flaming westbound sun, it brought relief from the furnace heat, but the rocks became his enemies, tripping and cutting his feet in the moonless black.

Perhaps it had always been in his heart to head towards Mount Sinai. Perhaps during those long lonely days an impression began to form in his heart, a magnet drawing him, pulling him, causing him to wonder if this was indeed the voice again. It couldn't be! He had failed miserably— he was a disgrace to God and Israel. And yet the tugging grew stronger, until he knew that not only should he go to Sinai, but he should go to the cave that Moses reputedly stood in when the Lord passed by so many years earlier. (The Hebrew text reveals that Elijah went to 'the' cave— presumably a reference to the Cave of Moses.) Could it possibly be that the God who had shown himself to the mighty Moses might actually do something similar for a washed-up suicidal depressive called Elijah?

It was but a tiny spark, a faint flicker of hope that glimmered in his heart but, like a man cupping a camp-fire flame, protecting it from the threatening wind, he nursed that hope carefully, and began the journey to the Mountain of Moses.

He took the westward road to Kadesh-Barnea, a town on the perimeter of the Sinai Desert, a last outpost of life before the dreadful dustbowl began. It was a place where men would thoroughly pick the minds of the local bed-ouins, frantically trying to gather information about trails and landmarks in the great Sinai. The very fact that Elijah would step out into the wilderness alone shows us some-thing of the urgent desperation of the man. He had to know the embrace of God again, so he was willing to launch out into a hauntingly deceptive place—a land of old ghosts where a whole nation got lost for two decades. Even the most desolate place is warmed by the presence of friends, fellow travellers. The Israelites of old wandered in the Sinai with God as their guide and with the comforting soundtrack of the voices and laughter of a crowd of millions.

As Elijah looked out across the powder-sky furnace that was Sinai, there must have been some natural apprehen-sion in his heart. Would the leather-lined faces of the Kadesh bedouins be the last human beings he would ever see? Would he become just another skeleton; an ugly skull-smile picked at by scavenger birds and jack-als; a monument to sober other travellers? Whatever the risk, he knew somehow that he had to do it, for life without God was living death, and Mount Sinai was his last, desperate hope.

So Elijah went out there alone. Six long weeks of empty wandering: searing heat in the morning, longing for the reliable relief of the afternoon breezes, disappointment as the sun dived for cover each day leaving the sharp chill of the night. Think of it! Translate yourself into his sandals: forty long days of trudging despair. This was no Cherith, for at Cherith there had been God, and though there was so much silence, it was a pregnant quiet; a purposeful isolation. Down through the trackless plain of Tih he went, stopping only to sleep and scoop under the sand to get yellowish water from the temails—life for those who knew where to look.

Those were the longest days of his life. Then he saw the chaotic mass of peaks that was Sinai, away in the distance—granite savagely slashing the brilliant blue sky. Perhaps then he knew the disappointment which seeps into us when we discover that most things are not quite as good as they were anticipated to be. Sinai was undeniably striking, quite beautiful, but just . . . ordinary. No cloud of glory. No booming voice of God. No dancing dramatic lightning bolts.

Perhaps he stood at the north end of the Plain of Rahah where Israel had gathered to hear Moses read the Law to Israel. Did he imagine the millions of his ancestors standing there, covenant-makers of history? Did he perhaps yell out the commandments, fascinated by the sound of his own voice echoing around the plateau, disappointed that the only voice he could hear was his own? What had happened to that other voice? Where had God gone?

Finally, after meandering around the mountain for days, he decided to climb higher and go to the cave where Moses was alleged to have resided when he spent forty days in communion with God. Scripture refers to it in the Kings narrative not just as 'a' cave, but as 'the' cave. Like a pilgrim at an ancient shrine, Elijah went in and lay down. It was all a waste—the journey had been futile.

He was at the most sacred spot he could imagine, and it was all too obvious. The God of Moses was gone.

Or so he thought.

*   *   *

Look at him, and wonder again. There he sits, hunched in the corner of a dingy cave gouged roughly out of the mountainside. The man who had stood in the finest home in Israel and rebuked the owner is holed up, seated on a carpet of dried bat's droppings; arms hugging his knees which are drawn up to his chest, foetal position. His face is buried, pressed down hard on knees and forearms, his knotted, bedraggled black hair a mop that almost touches the floor. No sound. Only the shuddering, shaking shoulders tell you that he is crying again. A man at the end of himself, starved of hope.

Can you identify with him, as he longs to rekindle life and faith, but doesn't know how? Have you wandered back to places—church buildings, cities, homes—where many years ago you possessed a simple trust in God that was so uncluttered and uncomplicated? Where is your Sinai?

For me, it is a small, functional park in Ilford, where I would spend every lunch break from the office. As a brand new Christian, I would go there each day and sit on the same bench with the warmth of the sun on my back, or in a shelter in the winter. There I eagerly devoured chapter after chapter of the Bible, revelling in the thrill of new discovery. Prayer was easy, and any struggle I put down to the fact that I was a 'new babe'. There were many questions, but it seemed so easy just to deal with anything that

I didn't understand by a quick shrug of the shoulders and a child-like prayer: 'Oh well, Lord, I'll just trust you anyway. . . .' It was first love—virginal, untouched by clever theological speculations and the erosion of cynicism. I didn't know back then that some preachers waxed eloquent on Sundays and loved other men's wives on Mondays. I didn't know about the churches which displayed 'God is love' posters on their buildings and then fought and gossiped and split, and did so in the name of God. No, back then, every Christian was still a wonderful, pure person; another member of my new family. My love was untainted by hypocrisy or disappointment. I had no experience of 'sheep shock'—the discovery that Christians fail and sin like everybody else. That park is my Sinai; the place where I first got acquainted with God.

I've been back to the park since, and wished that I hadn't discovered some of the things I know now; wished again for an innocent, simple faith. Words like 'ecclesiology' and 'eschatology', 'Calvinism' and 'Arminianism' just didn't exist. I knew nothing of soteriology. I just knew that I was saved. In the park, only one thing mattered: God was alive and he loved me. I wanted to change the world with Jesus, my brand new friend.

Perhaps your condition is far more serious, and you can relate to the Sinaitic caveman more closely. For you, God has become little more than a theory, a doctrinal idea, a cause, a reason for the morality programme that you call your Christianity. You attend church, and perhaps it's good, lively and creative, but it feels like going to a birthday party every week, only you forgot whose birthday it is. The truths that you have committed yourself to begin to sound like mere slogans. You knot your brow with intense concentration during the worship time, and do your best to imagine dark Calvary hillsides during communion, but perhaps you feel like this prophet. It's not that you can even blame your church, for it's widely regarded as a good church. But the question nags, the unspeakable gnawing: Where is God?

Where is the God of Elijah?

How to help a caveman

Be honest. What would you expect God to do with a man like this? Send his last pay cheque with a note of thanks? Send him a fireball and burn him up for being bad? Worse even than that, maybe just leave him alone, ignore him, let him die in the dampness of the cave? I'm grateful to God that I can report that the Almighty chose none of these available options. I'm still discovering that God is better and kinder than I ever imagined him to be. Perhaps that's one reason why eternity really does mean for ever and ever—so that God can show his 'immeasurable kindness to us in Christ Jesus'. The Lord knew just what Elijah needed.

God at Sinai 1: total truth-teller

It is truth that sets us free, particularly from fear, and as we've already noted, Elijah was labouring under an exaggerated perception of his problem. Fear has the ability to amplify and enlarge the size of real problems to a size way beyond their own. In some cases I have met Christians who have spent years in what can only be described as futile shadow-boxing—dodging and weaving and defending themselves against nothing more than the power of their own vivid imaginations. Of course, shadow-boxing can be just as demanding and exhausting as the real thing.

Fear became an obsessive part of Elijah's thought patterns. His mind was locked in fear—always walking down the same mental pathway, round and round in anxiety-filled circles. Ever heard a record stylus get stuck in the groove? Remember the infuriating repetitiveness, as one phrase or three notes are repeated over and over and over again, until mercifully someone taps the needle gently and moves it along to the next phrase of the song?

This was Elijah's mind. And so God asked the question: 'What are you doing here?' The question was to be asked again later. Look at Scripture, and you'll find that Elijah gave the Lord the exact same answer, word for word, twice over. Mentally, the stylus was stuck, and Elijah was on a railway track of predictable, well-worn thought processes that would ultimately drive him over the brink to the abyss of insanity—unless someone jogged the needle.

That is why God asked the question. Did God need an answer for his own benefit? No! Man looks on the outside, but God looks on the heart. The Lord wasn't asking for his own academic benefit.

The question was an invitation. 'Elijah! Talk to me! Spill your guts if you want to. Throw aside your nice pleasant speech and just tell me what's going on in that locked mind of yours.' God knew, but he wanted Elijah to get all those pent-up feelings of emotions out into the open; on the table if you like.

Elijah's response shows us that he was not afraid to speak his mind to God. Now remember, this man had seen nuclear-fission-type fire snap suddenly out of the heavens; he had stood back and watched the sizzling of the water being instantly evaporated by the white-hot heat that shot laser-like from the finger of God. He knew that he was dealing with someone of *real* power—one who could crumple the planet in his hand in a second and toss it aside like a spoiled paper—but still he spilled his guts.

Be honest with God. Tell him what you really think. He knows your heart anyway. Sometimes I think that we pray our poetic, flowing stanzas and it is as if God says, 'Oh, give me a break! Cut the long speech telling me what you think I want to hear. Just tell it the way it is!'

Beware of compulsive self-talk too. When I first became a Christian I was so desperate to do the will of God that I became obsessed with the fear of making a mistake. I bought books on the subject (and there were plenty available—it took me for ever to decide which ones it was God's will for me to read). I prayed, I fasted, I tried to work out the significance of my circumstances. I cross-examined my heart to check if I had real confirmatory peace. Peace, I was told, was supposed to supernaturally accompany every decision, like an umpire who confirms a call in sport. The scriptural basis for this was Colossians 3:15, where it says: 'Let the peace of Christ rule in your hearts.' Every book I read suggested that this meant that this subjective feeling should be the final indicator that all is well in God's sight. Quite apart from the fact that Colossians 3 is an exhortation on relational difficulties in the local church, and has nothing whatever to do with personal guidance, I was so terrified I might not have enough peace, that I was in a total state of panic anyway!

I asked other believers for advice—and my fear increased to a paralysing level. I was unable to make decisions lest I made a mistake and be consigned to the terrifying scrap heap unhelpfully designated by fiery preachers as 'God's second best'. A thousand times I travelled a well-worn mental trail, repeating over and over my reasons for what I was doing—particularly in challenging meetings. Looking back I feel that I came close to a breakdown. Someone had to jog the needle for me, and let me know that the will of God was not designed to be a baffling jigsaw puzzle with fiendish forfeits for those who make a mistake. But it was compulsive, almost obsessive thinking that got me into such a state. Such was the thinking of Elijah—hence God's kindly cross-examination.

The question was also a revelation: 'What are you doing here, Elijah?' God uses his servant's name. In some ways, that's natural enough—to use someone's name is an expression of tenderness and care. But remember the meaning of that name: Eli-yah—the Lord, he is the real God. Now rephrase that into the question. To a man in a self-imposed solitary confinement, miles from where he had been called to be, crumpled by despair, terrified by thoughts of suicide, God says: 'What are you doing here, the Lord, he is the real God?'

God knows the power of gentle, subtle irony, but judging by his servant's response, the pun was too subtle for Elijah.

God at Sinai 2: an invitation to choose

God is speaking. Elijah sits still, fixed, unmovable, unresponsive. So a cosmic firework display begins. Scripture records that 'God was not in' the wind, earthquake and fire that follow—but he did allow this eruption of attention-grabbing natural phenomena to break out. I'm amazed at the faith of Elijah on Carmel. I'm even more stunned at his hard-hearted attitude on Sinai.

First of all a hurricane-level wind of unprecedented strength whips up, and it is so mighty that it breaks rocks. Now Elijah's cave becomes a wind tunnel, his hair a mane standing on end, his cloak a flag whipped and reeled around his legs. Naturally speaking, it's hardly surprising that Elijah stays put, for the cave would have offered some protection from the terrifying blast, but God had said: 'Come out—I'm here.' Was this a reminder to Elijah that he had been called to obedience, even if it meant a lifetime spent facing the winds of popular opinion, the hurricanes of murderous threats of powerful men and women smashing into his face? It is current practice to give powerful storms a name: Hugo, for example. Elijah had been called to stand firm in the face of hurricane Jezebel (a serious blast of hot air if ever there was one) and had failed. He stays put in his cave, battered by the storm and six paces from God's embrace. All he has to do is step out. . . .

Stage two of the display begins now. Just when the prophet begins to feel relief because the terrifying winds are beginning to subside, a stomach-churning earthquake begins. Now this really is a prod from God. Evacuate, Elijah! Get out of there! You shouldn't hang around in caves during an earthquake—they might cave in.

The ground trembles and churns and boils, and the only song Elijah can sing is his very own version of 'We shall not, we shall not be moved'. His will withstands the voice of God, the mighty wind and the restless upheaval of the earth. He's not coming out.

Stage three, the final scenario: fire. Familiar territory this, throwing up memories of the Carmel that was just weeks earlier, but had seemed like years ago—or had it really happened? Did Elijah go through that doubt-amnesia that causes us to question even the greatest examples of God's grace and intervention in our lives? Just as the bolt from the Carmel blue had been designed to confirm the reality of the true, living God to an entire nation, so this personal fire licks thirstily around the cave specifically to confirm the struggling faith of one lonely man.

Wind that turned the desert into a sand-blaster. The earth in convulsions. Furnace-hot flames out of thin air. And one stationary Elijah, who still won't venture out.

Then a voice speaks inside that cave, and the voice succeeds where all the other natural displays failed. Was God showing Elijah that the ability to hear the voice of God is greater than the ability to take authority over the forces of nature? God was about to speak, and declare a strategy that would succeed where the fire of Carmel had failed. We will never know what God said in that moment—Scripture only records that he spoke, not the words that he said.

I've speculated at great length why it is that no more detail is recorded, considering the fact that the word or words God spoke succeeded in convincing Elijah that he really ought to obey Yahweh and walk five steps to the mouth of the cave. Perhaps despite the stark focus in which Elijah's downfall is portrayed, God determined to pull a veil of privacy over this most intimate moment of his friendship with his man.

Whatever the dialogue, it worked. Elijah made his choice: it was time to stop pouting, finish the pity party and start talking to God again.

God is omnipresent. The theologians define that as meaning that he is everywhere all of the time, and that, presumably, includes caves. God was in there with Elijah—so why invite the prophet to step outside 'because my presence is passing by'? Why not light up the musty darkness with a divine sparkler, or scrawl, 'I'm here, with love,' on the damp wall?

The call to come outside had nothing to do with location. It was an invitation to choose; to take a step; to engage the will. It was make your mind up time. Granted, God baited the invitation very heavily with an almost irresistible wooing: 'The presence of the Lord is passing by. . . .' The God of Cherith, Zarephath, Carmel, and yes Elijah, even Samaria with its whore-groves (where you could rent a prostitute who would tell you that you were doing the gods a service as well as yourself): that God of *everywhere* was passing by. But despite the heavy incentive programme, fundamentally this was all about choices.

The God of wind, earthquakes and fire can do all manner of incredible things. He can cause a colourful universe to jump into existence, just because he says so. He can instruct the sun to stand still in time and space for an hour or two. He can listen and respond to the hearts of millions of his praying people, all at the same time. He can hire and fire kings and princes as he chooses, and weave a plan to redeem idiot mankind through what seemed like a fly-blown execution outside the city walls of Jerusalem. When it comes to miracle working and making the impossible spring into reality, God has an impressive track record.

Yet there's one thing he cannot, will not do.

He won't make our minds up for us. He won't overrule the dignity and depravity of the human will. We always have a choice. That's why there is a hell, because to the very end, God refuses to dehumanise the crown of his creation, mankind, by taking away his right to choose, and that commitment is eternal. Not even the delights of heaven will be forced into the clenched fists of a man or a woman who has decided that he or she doesn't want to be around God, period. Ironically, hell is the last monument to the uniqueness of the human being, for forgiveness will not be force fed.

Only when Elijah stepped out did God give some

further instruction and strategy: Elijah's will had to respond before the next steps could be revealed.

I have seen too many Christians almost destroy their lives because they refused to make the right choices. Some of them have been through hours of deliverance and counselling ministry, have responded to 10,000 altar calls and have given the impression that they really do want God to have his way in their lives, but in the final analysis, they haven't engaged their will. Such is the case with one man I know who has attended a lively evangelical church for many years—and still has a huge problem with pornography and prostitutes. Every time I see him I hear the same story: 'I know that I need to do the right thing, Jeff, and I will, eventually. . . .' But the years go by and his spiritual arteries are hardening. Every time I see him, not only is he still in his cave, but it gets darker and more forbidding. God has not let him down—he just won't take five steps.

Perhaps those of us who live this way feel that if God really wants us to shape up, then he'll shout loud enough to make us jump. Or maybe he'll wave a flag, pick us up by the ears and spin us around, or . . . blow some wind, shake the planet, send down some fire. . . .

Yet God 'is not in' all of that. His voice is described in this passage as 'the still, small voice'. Some have translated this as 'the sound of gentle silence'. It is '*qol demama daqqa*', the silent sound.

Silent sound? Seems like a contradictory statement—like black white, rich poor or live dead. Silent sound. It seems to me in my experience that the voice of God is just like that: gentle, calm, solidly there, yet—was that really him? How many times have you thought that you heard God speak, only to spend the next few days considering whether the actual source was your imagination/a curry you had the night before/the devil/wishful thinking? No wonder John Wimber remarks (and I paraphrase) that God is saying a lot to us—we don't seem to hear because he doesn't speak in a way we expect him to. Preconceptions about the nature of his voice ultimately cause us to become deaf to him.

Perhaps we don't hear him more because we are looking for him to say something new, when actually he may well be bringing us back to a previous statement that we've ignored or disobeyed. Certainly that was Elijah's experience. Once out of the cave, cloak wrapped round his face for fear that he might actually see Yahweh, it's question time again: 'What are you doing here, Elijah?'

Same old question. Back to square one. Sometimes we feel as if God has gone silent on us. Perhaps it's good to check to make sure that last time he spoke, we heard and responded.

God at Sinai 3: incredible radical

Having finally captured Elijah's attention, it was time for God to reveal his strategy. What a plan it was too! It was a totally radical approach—so revolutionary that Elijah had missed it altogether. Elijah thought God's plan was to cause Ahab and Jezebel to repent and that the nation would follow, but as we've already noted, God was finished with them.

God's Plan B went like this:

Step one: 'Go back the way you came, and go to the Desert of Damascus. When you get there, anoint Hazael king over Aram.'

Whether Elijah realised it or not, this was designed to solve the problem of Ahab and Jezebel. The Arameans were called to wage a war upon Israel behind which flashed the judgement of God; a war in which the King of Israel would be killed, and Israel would receive punishment for their awful, heartless and idolatrous crimes. Hazael would become nothing but a puppet to fulfil the will of God. If Elijah would obey, then the plan would be set in motion.

Step two: 'Also, anoint Jehu son of Nimshi king over Israel.'

Elijah would have been shattered, staggered even, to hear this part of God's great idea. This was unbelievable. Perhaps he had at last been driven over the abyss into madness. Why had he fled in terror in the first place? Because he was scared of Ahab and Jezebel. And now listen to God's instruction: 'Anoint another king!' Nothing could be more guaranteed to ignite the raging demonic anger of Jezebel to inferno pitch. To anoint Jehu would be to sign his own death warrant—or so it seemed to Elijah.

History shows us clearly what Elijah could never know, except by faith. He didn't know that Jehu was a man with a heart for renewal and revival. He didn't know that Jehu was destined to give the order for Jezebel to be thrown out of a high window to her timely death. He didn't know that Jehu was destined to be the man who oversaw the systematic execution of every single one of Ahab's seventy surviving male descendants, so that the cursed dynasty would never rise again. He didn't know that it would be Jehu who would throw the Tyrian Baal out of Israel, and that even though Jehu would later compromise himself, he was the instrument of God to bring about a massive reform in Israel. Elijah didn't know all this. . . .

Step three: 'And anoint Elisha son of Shaphat from Abel Meholah to succeed you as prophet. Jehu will put to death any who escape the sword of Hazael, and Elisha will put to death any who escape the sword of Jehu.'

Having given his strategy for the nation, God now turns

to Elijah's personal need—primarily, his need of a friend, a successor; someone whom he could shape so that the prophetic anointing could continue. The next chapter deals with the relationship between these two in more detail.

Step four: A final encouraging word to the man who had thrown a forty-day pity party: 'Yet I reserve seven thousand in Israel—all whose knees have not bowed down to Baal and all whose mouths have not kissed him.'

Again, God was confirming the truth: Elijah had stood bravely, but not alone. He was to be encouraged by the fact that there was still a faithful remnant who were true to God. He was not the Lone Ranger after all.

So Plan B, God's plan, had been given. The big question is: Did Elijah obey?

The answer is not, as they say, 'Yes and no.' It is more accurately, 'No . . . and no . . . and yes.'

He didn't anoint Hazael. That would come later, under the ministry of Elisha, and he indeed would become instrumental in the justice programme that God insisted was appropriate for Israel. But it wasn't Elijah who anointed Hazael.

This disobedience is so shocking that evangelical commentators have been loath to concede that Elijah actually got it wrong. The classic writer A. W. Pink actually suggests in his otherwise wonderful book on Elijah* that only 'infidels' would suggest that Elijah made a mistake in not holding an anointing service. He argues that Elisha did it eventually, and so that was sufficient.

But what did God say? 'Go back the way you came . . . to the Desert of Damascus. *When you get there, anoint Hazael*.' Now that's very specific and clear, isn't it?

---

* A.W. Pink, *The Life of Elijah* (Banner of Truth Trust), p 246.

Pink argues that perhaps Elijah did anoint Hazael, but the Bible doesn't record it—although it does carefully document the way Elijah initiated Elisha into the office of prophet by throwing his cloak around him. It isn't enough to say that David was anointed twice, so perhaps Hazael was too. In David's case, *both* anointings are clearly documented in Scripture.

Also, if Hazael was anointed secretly by Elijah, why didn't he immediately become King of Aram, as he did when Elisha anointed him? Why did Elisha, years later, announce to Hazael that 'the Lord had shown him' Hazael was to become King, if they had both been involved in a secret anointing ceremony in the Desert of Damascus years earlier? And why did Hazael react with such amazement and surprise when Elisha prophesied that he would be King?

The unpalatable fact seems to be that Elijah didn't follow through on stage one.

Moving to stage two, the anointing of Jehu, the answer is 'no' again. And so the evil reign of Ahab continued unabated, and when he was mercifully killed during battle (a stray Aramean arrow finished him off), Hazael was not on the scene, and Jehu wasn't there, anointed and ready to take over.

Ahab's son, Ahaziah, ruled for two years. Scripture is terse and brief in describing him: 'He was just like his father.' Two more years of the Baals. There would be a brief moment towards the end of Elijah's ministry when the old prophet would challenge the Baal worship by calling down fire upon 100 of Jehoram's soldiers, and Elijah also prophesied Ahaziah's death—but when that demise came as a result of the King taking a fatal tumble from his Samarian balcony, there was no Jehu waiting in the wings, ready and willing to take the throne. He had not been anointed.

So another descendant of Ahab ascends to the throne. Another son, in fact. This time it was Jehoram—not to be confused with Jehoram of Judah, who became evil by marrying Athaliah, one of Ahab and Jezebel's daughters! Elijah sent a prophetic note across the border to him, condemning him to a painful death of rotting intestines.

Jehoram of Israel was a little better than his brother, but not much. Some minor amendments were made (probably because he was scared stiff that what had happened to his brother and brother-in-law might happen to him). But his eleven-year reign was inconsequential, and he was destined to die at the hands of the next king. During Jehoram's reign Elijah was called away to heaven.

And so thirteen years were wasted. God's radical plan was not totally thwarted—it was just delayed. But the shadow of Ahab's dynasty continued to eclipse Israel.

Then, one great day, the sun broke out. Elisha, now in the full throes of his prophetic office, declared that *God* had shown him Hazael was to become King over Aram. (No suggestion here that Elijah had told Elisha many years earlier. God had to speak his strategy again!)

It was Elisha who summoned up the bravery to anoint Jehu, right under the nose of the then reigning Jehoram. Elisha was willing to go the full distance with Plan B— and so Jehu ascended to the throne.

The sad implication of all this is that Elijah was a great, mighty, anointed man, but one who was unwilling to go all the way with God when it came to being utterly radical. He saw and experienced so much of the Lord, and dwarfs us by comparison with his great bravery and faith. But the fact remains that he didn't follow through 100%—the threefold strategy of Plan B was met by a mixed response: 'No, no and yes.'

The radical had reached his limits.

Lessons from the cave

There is an obvious and vital lesson for us to learn from this part of Elijah's story: we too will be tempted to become limited radicals, who talk the language of radical commitment and change, but hold back when it comes to following through on what God is saying. I believe that such an attitude is the reason for the decline of the charismatic renewal in Britain. The seventies were heady days for many of us who were leading denominational churches. The winds of change were blowing, forcing us to look again at the way in which we structured our churches, appointed leaders, acted towards women leaders. Services of community singing were replaced with a real thirst for a genuine worship experience. We struggled to replace services with meetings, and began to realise just how much of the spirit of religion had affected us, because instead of being founded on clear New Testament principles (*sola biblica*, the Bible alone) we were *sola traditiona*! It was a painful but exhilarating time as many of us searched our hearts, eager to do whatever it took to allow God to have the church his way.

Yet I wonder whether we became enamoured with the symptoms of renewalism rather than the root. The heart of renewal is the throne of God being established in his church—the firm establishment of kingdom rather than democratic, institutional or hierarchical rule. But soon there were certain obvious criteria which declared that you were part of a renewed church. An overhead projector was mandatory equipment, accompanied of course by thousands of transparencies of the latest praise and worship songs. We changed our names from 'Gruntsville Baptist/Pentecostal/Anglican Church' to 'Gruntsville Christian Fellowship', ripped out the pews and put the chairs in a circle, jumped up and down during worship times and liberally sprinkled our conversations with the latest charismatic terminology. No wonder a leading bishop appeared on a BBC radio programme and began (inadvertently) to discuss the 'cosmetic' renewal. Because, for all that, the fundamental *structure* of the British church remains unchanged—we still live with the unbiblical notion of a clergy/laity divide, which is indefensible in New Testament terms. The Berlin Wall may have fallen, but the Stained Glass Wall stands strong!

The renewal profoundly affected individuals' lives, bringing a season of personal refreshing, and certainly there were some considerable changes of style—but did we go far enough? Or were we tempted to play it safe, bowing to popular opinion or institutional pressure? Did we establish God's throne, or did we just move the furniture around a bit? Are we experiencing what Gerald Coates and others have described as 'post-charismatic depression' because we too thought that the anointing of Hazael and Jehu was a great and wonderful idea—only we stopped short of actually doing it?

Perhaps we need what God told Elijah to initiate: a total reform of the power structure—another Reformation.

*   *   *

His mind was swimming with a mixture of excitement and fear. A return journey of hundreds of miles lay before him, but now he knew two things for sure: God was smiling upon him once more, and he was never again to endure the excruciating pain of a solo lifestyle. It was time to find Elisha. Time to pour out his heart to the younger man, so that he would be able to continue to hold the standard high. Of course there was the matter of the other anointings, but they would come later. . . .

8

After Sinai

While Elijah's public ministry and involvement in the ongoing life of Israel continued very spasmodically after he came down from Carmel, his contribution and effectiveness as a national prophet were never fully regained—perhaps a further indication that he had not totally obeyed God's instructions. This is not to say that his life was without significance after coming down from the mountain of Moses, for his ministry veered into other, fruitful directions. Elijah and Elisha probably spent a few years investing themselves in a prophetic school, training and shaping others. (We'll look more into that idea in the next chapter.) But the fact is that Elijah faded quickly from the national scene as a direct prophetic spokesman, and he only ministered publicly twice (and sent one prophecy through the postal system) in a period of between ten and fifteen years.

These years were turbulent times for Israel. During this period, the royal city of Samaria came under siege from Ben-Hadad of Syria, who held the nation to ransom and demanded that Ahab hand over his huge treasury of silver and gold, together with 'the best of his wives and children'. Amazingly, Ahab agreed to these terms, and only kicked up a fuss when Ben-Hadad increased his demands and insisted that Ahab's furniture be thrown in as part of the deal as well! ('Take my wife if you like, but touch my sofa and I'll break your face. . . .')

Obviously a prophetic voice was needed at this time of threat and calamity—but it was not the voice of Elijah that spoke during this national crisis. Scripture simply declares that 'a prophet came to Ahab and announced . . . '. This was probably one of the younger prophets from one of the colleges or 'schools of the prophets' that were gradually being re-established at this time.

There then followed a battle which included the mustering of some 7,000 Israelite men and was won largely because (a) God helped, and (b) Ben-Hadad and his friends were too busy partying to be a serious strategic threat. At the moment of truth, the King and the other thirty-two kings who had allied themselves with him were so 'tanked up' that they were almost totally oblivious to who and where the enemy was. No tactical brilliance was therefore required of the Israelites, as the enemy troops scored an own goal by turning upon one another in confusion, and destroyed themselves by the do-it-yourself method!

After this victory, the anonymous prophet went again to the palace and told Ahab to strengthen and consolidate his defences, warning of another attack to come in the following spring. But still there is nothing but silence from Tishbe, home of Elijah.

The young prophet was certainly accurate in his prediction, for spring blossomed and with it came another attack from Ben-Hadad, who had been falsely advised that Yahweh was only the god of the hills, and not the plains. Ben-Hadad's strategy was, 'We shall fight them on the plains—and beat them!' Of course, bad theology is a harsh taskmaster. Yahweh is the God of the universe. The opposition suffered massive casualties in just one day of fighting. Even those who escaped the battlefield met disaster—thousands were killed when the main wall of the city of Aphek fell upon them.

Ahab, however, was always a sucker for making unwise treaties. Instead of dealing with Ben-Hadad once and for all, he entered into a trading covenant with the man, and this caused God to break out yet another unnamed prophet. Indeed, God's anger was so stirred that one of the prophets was called to prophetically sentence the King of Israel to death because he 'set free a man [God] determined should die'. However, it wasn't Elijah who stepped forward to don the judge's black cap, but rather one of the 'sons of the prophets' (1 Kings 20:35).

Through all of this national and international upheaval, Elijah is silent. So apart from his work behind the scenes, what *did* he do publicly during those fifteen years?

1. The 'framing' of Naboth

The Naboth conspiracy took place some five or six years after the Sinai theophany. Nothing had changed at the palace: evil still lingered unchallenged in the hearts of the royal couple. Carmel had momentarily stirred and disturbed Ahab, but not for long. Like water off the proverbial duck's back, he had brushed his eye-witness encounter with truth and power aside. He and Jezebel determined to continue their selfish, hedonistic lifestyles, ignorant or oblivious to Yahweh.

Yet while nothing had changed, all was not well with Ahab. In fact the King was having one of his customary sulking sessions—one which had driven him to his bed with depression. He was refusing to eat—a pouting prince with his thumb in his mouth. The reason for his childish, petulant behaviour was Naboth: a man of integrity who at least had some level of respect for the true God and refused to sell his vineyard to the King, despite the offer of a fair price or a replacement vineyard. Naboth knew that such a deal was tempting as a business contract, but it violated God's law: 'No inheritance in Israel is to pass from tribe to tribe, for every Israelite shall keep the tribal land inherited from his forefathers' (Num 36:7).

Enter the spider. Jezebel was staggered by her husband's behaviour. What kind of King would allow his moods or actions to be controlled by a nobody like Naboth? She had a plan. And once again, the demons smiled on her. It was executed with brilliant efficiency. It was a glorious set-up, with a little help from her friends, both seen and unseen.

*   *   *

Naboth was confused by the whirl of events, but thrilled and excited all the same. He had been somewhat nervous about declining the King's offer, and he had worried for some while about possible reprisals or harassment. But now it seemed his fears were groundless. Apparently, the King had decided to honour Naboth's integrity. All over Jezreel copies of a royal edict were pinned, proclaiming a special fast in honour of Naboth. Think of it! Him, a humble nobody, being invested with honour by the King and Queen of the land. The plan was to seat him in a place of honour with the elders of the town, and there the whole city would gather to pay tribute to him.

Naboth shook his head with amazement. It was like a dream; almost too good to be true. He looked at the sea of smiling faces, a wave of approval for him . . . too good to be true?

*   *   *

The crowd that had been cheering seconds ago were hushed into an awkward, embarrassed silence. From the back of the packed town square, the voices of two men were raised— their bony fingers pointing up towards the platform of honour, where a man who had been so happy and proud just seconds ago now sat white faced, with skin taut and eyes wide. 'He cursed God and King! He's a traitor, and deserves to die.'

The crowds knew. They knew that it wasn't true; that Naboth was a good, honest man. They also knew that the accusers were scoundrels; thugs in the pay of someone very, very powerful. But what could they do? Solemnly, the elders of the town, who had found themselves somewhat richer in the last few hours courtesy of the palace, stood and condemned the man whom they had just honoured to be taken out and stoned to death. The crowds stood silent, every man wanting to shout, to protest, to *do* something. But they said nothing.

The now-screaming Naboth was led away, probably already a madman because of the soaring joy and the plummeting agony of the day. Away, to face the pelting of the stones that would crack and break and bruise and bloody his frail body, until finally the aches that screamed from every cell within him would be mercifully silenced. And then they took the dead man's sons and stoned them to death as well, so that there would be no legal inheritance complications to prevent 'an unknown backer' from purchasing Naboth's fateful vineyard. It was a bad job well done.

Poor Naboth had been right.

It was too good to be true.

At the palace, a glad and smiling King got up from his tear-stained bed. He washed and dressed and celebrated with a sumptuous meal, and blessed the day that his father had arranged his marriage to the fair lady Jezebel.

*   *   *

I wonder whether Elijah agonised over the shift in his ministry away from the glare of public profile. During those six long years of silence, did he ever wistfully reminisce over the 'glory days' of national significance? Did he ever wonder if he was now consigned to the scrap heap of half-obedience—a blazing sword in the hand of God once, now feeling like a blunt stick; yesterday's news? What kind of agonies come to those who have stood in the spotlight of fame, recognition or influence, who suddenly find that the stage lights have dimmed, the scenery has rotted and faded, and the auditorium is empty—the crowds have gone, and they've taken their intoxicating applause with them? All that's left are yellowing posters and a few dated photographs. It's interesting that during the Naboth narrative Elijah is referred to as 'Elijah, the prophet from Tishbe'—almost as if a reintroduction is necessary. He has gone back home to the humble village where it all started; obscurity again. . . .

However, like Samson, whose hair began to grow again, and had one last burst of blessing before death, so Elijah is destined to blaze a trail one more time before handing over the job to one younger and stronger. The King must be rebuked—justice must be done. The oppressed must be defended. And Elijah must tread finally and totally upon the very thing that he feared.

He had to go to the palace again.

Something of God's mercy and kindness can be seen in this recommissioning of Elijah. Even though it seems he was unwilling to go all the way, yet still God enabled him to recover some of his confidence by providing him with a mission that he would be able to respond to fully. It was, after all, familiar ground as he had confronted Ahab face to face before. The stage would be lit, albeit temporarily, a couple more times.

*　　*　　*

It was the joy that comes when you get something new, or when you reach a goal: a quiet, luscious sense of satisfaction. So Ahab felt as he strolled regally around the 'Traitor's' Vineyard—now the title deeds for the place were safely in the royal purse. Like a child who has screamed and begged and manipulated until he has finally got his own way, and then smiles with self-congratulation, so Ahab smiled. Briefly.

Suddenly the vines parted behind him, and a voice bellowed out, insistent and throaty, demanding a response. The King turned around, a sense of *déjà vu* causing his mind to spin too.

He knew that voice, but it was a sound from the past—an uncomfortable echo from yesteryear. No, it couldn't be. . . .

Ahab looked into the face of his old enemy. Elijah.

It was a prophetic curse. Rhythmic, lilting, haunting even: *'Haratzachta vegam yarashta!'* The closest English translation, according to Lance Pierson, is, 'So you're a con man as well as a cut throat!'

This was the third slap in the face that Ahab received from God: a slap with a drought because of spiritual idolatry; a rebuke with a suspended death sentence for his disobedience and rashness in covenant-making with demonised kings; and now, a smack once more for oppressing the poor. It's worth pausing for a moment here to take note of the fact that God is interested in both the political and the so-called spiritual. With God, there is no distinction. Those who would like the church to confine itself to the winning of souls only and to be silent in matters of politics, have neglected to read Scripture. Yet such a dualistic viewpoint ('concentrate on the spiritual, ignore the secular') still pervades. In an environment where the church practises a pathological fear of all things politically controversial, we will never be able to cry out on behalf of the poor and oppressed—and my Bible tells me that the gospel is primarily for them. Oppression and injustice cause the heart of God to rage with terrifying anger—and they should make us angry as well. We need to mix genuine caring compassion with our activism. When we cease to defend the rights of the oppressed, we become a hard-faced group of moralists—passionate about our agendas, but with no heart. No wonder there are social analysts who have declared the so-called Moral Majority or Christian Right in the USA to be dead. As one of their own leaders confessed, 'We had an agenda, but no compassion.'

With love and tears, but with strategy and clarity, the church must say to governments, to certain multi-national corporations, and indeed to all who oppress: *'Haratzachta vegam yarashta!'* (Or, more helpfully, a contemporary and more understandable version thereof!) As love and truth mingle, then the church becomes the incarnate conscience that God has surely called her to be.

*   *   *

Ahab, now instantly robbed of the joy that he had felt as the new master of the vineyard, immediately tried to distract Elijah with a few cunning, well-chosen words: 'Have you caught up with me, my enemy?'

After the long years, Ahab immediately drew thick verbal battle lines afresh, invoking memories of Jezebel's vow of long ago—a vow that made Elijah an enemy still. Is there perhaps a hint of mockery here too, in the question, 'Have you caught up with me?'? Perhaps he was taunting the prophet who had been sheltering in obscurity for too long—'Where have you been, Elijah? Long time no see! After all these years, you've finally managed to find me.'

Elijah didn't flinch. He made no attempt to explain himself; to justify his long silence. He just launched into the bad news (there was no good news available for Ahab at this stage of his reprobate life). After denouncing the King as one who had 'sold himself' (as one who sells himself utterly into slavery) to do evil in God's sight, Elijah delivered a sentence in two counts. Let's take a time-warp approach so we can see the power of the prophetic utterance more clearly:

Part one—the promise: 'I am going to bring disaster on you. I will consume your descendants and cut off from Ahab every last male in Israel—slave or free. I will make your house like that of Jeroboam son of Nebat and that of Baasha son of Ahijah, because you have provoked me to anger and have caused Israel to sin' (1 Kings 21:21–22).

The fulfilment: About twelve years later, Jehu would instigate a purge that would let everyone know that 'not a word spoken against the house of Ahab will fail'. The seventy remaining descendants of Ahab, together with all his chief men, close friends and priests would all be put to the sword, their heads put in baskets and sent to Jezreel.

Then all the relatives of Ahab's son Ahaziah would be slaughtered by the well of Beth Eked—forty-two of them.

Finally, Jehu was destined to go to Samaria, and wipe out any and every remaining member of Ahab's family—a thorough and total purge. God means what he says.

Part two—the promise: 'Dogs will devour Jezebel by the wall [or plot of ground] of Jezreel. Dogs will eat those belonging to Ahab who die in the city, and the birds of the air will feed on those who die in the country' (1 Kings 21:23–24).

This wasn't the first time dogs had been used as agents by God to judge royalty. Elijah prophesied that Ahab's house would be like Jeroboam's and Baasha's houses. Jeroboam had already gone down in history as an idolater whose descendants were eaten by dogs. It is written of Jeroboam: 'The Lord struck him down and he died' (2 Chron 13:20). The very mention of his name would have brought an icy chill to Ahab's heart—a reminder from contemporary history that God would perform what he had said.

Then, the mention of Baasha drove the point home like a sharp knife. He was another one who had received the canine treatment: 'Dogs will eat those belonging to Baasha who die in the city.'

The fulfilment: Again, it would be some twelve years

later. By this time Ahab would be dead, succeeded by his evil son Ahaziah, with Jezebel as Queen Mother. She would have known that the end had come as Jehu walked through the gates of the Jezreel country house. News had reached her that Jehu had just killed Ahaziah. The great purge had begun. She did her manipulative best to save her own neck, painting her eyes and fixing her hair (perhaps she could use her old charms seductively one last time). When the beauty treatment failed, she even tried a last attempt at undermining Jehu, yelling out of the window at him, 'Have you come in peace, Zimri, you murderer of your master?' This 'Zimri' is not mentioned anywhere else in biblical history, so we must assume that he was simply a contemporary figure who was infamous for his treachery. This was a bit of name calling on the part of the desperate Queen Mother.

It was a doomed scheme, however. She was thrown out of the high window by a couple of her own servants who swiftly decided that it would be politically expedient to be nice to Jehu! Considering the evil smear that was Jezebel's life, it is worth reporting the details of her demise in full—macabre and sickening though they are:

So they threw her down, and some of her blood spattered the wall and the horses as they trampled her underfoot . . . when they went out to bury her, they found nothing except her skull, her feet and her hands. They went back and told Jehu, who said, 'This is the word of the Lord that he spoke through his servant Elijah the Tishbite: On the plot of ground at Jezreel dogs will devour Jezebel's flesh. Jezebel's body will be like refuse on the ground in the plot at Jezreel, so that no-one will be able to say, "This is Jezebel"' (2 Kings 9:33, 35–37).

*   *   *

When Ahab heard Elijah's words, he knew he was a dead man walking—and incredibly, for once in his life, he repented. It was a thorough job; one that, perhaps even more surprisingly, God responded to warmly. He tore his clothes, fasted, lay in sackcloth and 'went around meekly'. And after all the evil, the child killing, the moral scum of Ahab's life, God showed him a measure of mercy, determining that judgements would fall on his house rather than on him directly. The disaster was delayed by his repentant heart.

What a God we serve, who seizes on even a glimmer of repentance and shows mercy wherever and whenever he can! But this is not a 'happy ever after' story for Ahab. Within three short years he had gone back to his old ways, despising God's prophets and surviving again by political manipulation. Ahab's downfall was that he seemed unable or unwilling to learn his lessons, and so he seemed to go around in ever-vicious circles. He would realise the truth for a while, but then slip back into old patterns, never bringing his will into line with what he knew to be right.

The battle that had raged for years between Elijah and Ahab was over—they were never to meet again. Judgement day for this prince of evil came on the battlefield. A 'stray' Aramean arrow penetrated his armour, and despite being propped up in his chariot for the rest of the day (a last desperate propaganda exercise), he died from the massive loss of blood that 'spilled onto the floor of his chariot'.

They took the royal chariot to the splendid palace at Samaria—Ahab's old ivory tower. There they washed it in the prostitutes' pool in the palace grounds, where all battle weapons and chariots were taken for cleaning.

And Scripture notes one further little detail.

The dogs came by, and licked up his blood.

2. Elijah and Ahaziah

Ahab was gone, but still Elijah had not anointed Jehu, God's man for the hour. And so Ahab's son, a chip off the demonised block, came to power. He didn't enjoy an easy reign. Moab, the subject kingdom which lay east of the Jordan, had decided that it had had enough of Israel's tax demands. For some forty-six years Moab had been required to contribute 100,000 lamb fleeces and 100,000 ram skins every year to Israel's treasury. This was a massively heavy burden. So they staged a revolution, and rebelled against their oppressors. Apparently it didn't occur to King Ahaziah to seek the Lord—and so, like Daddy before him, he bowed the knee to the Baals.

The situation came to a head about four years after the Naboth incident, following a domestic accident which left the King injured with no casualty ward in sight for a few thousand years. He fell off his own balcony. How, or why, Scripture doesn't tell us. Some have speculated that he did so in a drunken stupor. Whatever the cause of his little fall, the effect was serious. He was badly injured, and so hurriedly sent a messenger off to Ekron, which had an extensive population of fortune-tellers. It was the insect god Baal-Zebub from whom he sought counsel. He didn't seek healing, but revelation. His question was simple: 'Will I live, or will I die?'

Enter the angel of the Lord, calling Elijah to active service once more. The King of Israel had especially offended Yahweh by consulting with Baal-Zebub, chief demon of demons, the lord of the flies, the god of the dung heap. The incredulity that reverberated in the heart of Yahweh is echoed three times in the call of Elijah, as he cries out to a King wallowing in refuse and sewage, 'Is there no God in Israel?'

The verdict was stark and stern. Elijah had intercepted Ahaziah's messengers as they urged their horses on towards Philistia's dung heap. They had wondered why they had felt compelled to stop at the beckoning of the leather-faced man, just another bedouin peasant, but they had stopped anyway. And then they understood. It was Elijah, the man who had become a thorn in the now dead Ahab's side. He had come out of obscurity again, to give the new King trouble. His message was bad news: no invitation to the King to repent; no drought to bring him to his senses. As a son of Ahab he should have known better. His father had been a pictorial illustration of depravity, and his mother was still yet the lingering black widow who loved the fly god. There was no room for misunderstanding in Elijah's words: 'Tell the King he will die.'

The King was understandably taken aback by the rude intervention of his father's old enemy, but there was no response of thoughtful repentance, in the hope that God might hold out some hope of reprieve as he had offered, without success, to Ahab. Instead he decided to fight—to fight Elijah. And to pick a fight with Elijah was to pick a fight with the living God, who is, as Hebrews 12:28-29 puts it, 'a consuming fire'.

The mounted commando unit had been carefully briefed for the mission. Some of the younger, more headstrong among them had laughed at the fact that fifty of their number—fifty of the élite troop in the land—were required for the arrest of just one man. They were eager, excited, ready to get into a mission that had a certain guarantee of success. But there were some who were unable to hide the pensive feelings that filled their hearts. They were old enough to remember Elijah from the glory days. The story of Carmel had been part of the

fabric of their childhood, and however limited their understanding, they knew that the man had some kind of power.
But this was not a time for fearful questioning. Orders had
been issued. There was a job to be done.

*   *   *

Some people wish that the next part of Elijah's story had
never been written. The facts are blunt, and somewhat
hideous. Elijah and Elisha were camped out on a hillside: a sure vantage point from where he would be able
to see all comers. The captain of the royal commando
issued a command to the man of God: 'This is what the
King says, "Come down at once!"'

Elijah's response was pointed, and the macabre miracle
that followed even more so. 'If I am a man of God,' he
said, 'may fire come down from heaven and consume you
and your fifty men!' The unpalatable fact is this: an instant
cremation took place. White-hot heat that vaporised flesh
flashed from the sky, incinerating the entire platoon in a
second—an eerie explosion without a bang. Like the
divine ignition that broke out against the moaning Israelites at Taberah (Num 11:3) and then again during the
rebellion of Korah, when 250 became smouldering
remains in an instant, so God decisively detonated the
arrogant captain and his men.

As if this wasn't enough, the whole process is then
repeated. The incredibly pig-headed Ahaziah sent out
another posse on what proved to be a kamikaze mission,
because they met exactly the same fate. One hundred
smouldering mounds and the foul, sickly odour of

scorched flesh were all that remained to testify that these crack fighters had ever existed.

Back at the palace, Ahaziah sat unmoved, and sent out platoon number three. The commander of the third outfit was a little more sensible than his charcoaled comrades in leadership. He fell on his knees before Elijah and pleaded for mercy—a somewhat unusual military strategy. At this point the angel of God returns and assures Elijah that it would be safe for him to go with the officer and confront the bull-headed King face to face. The meeting is hurriedly arranged, and Ahaziah holds the most depressing audience of his life. Elijah simply marches in and repeats the word already spoken; 'Yes, King—you are still going to die.' And he did—after a reign of less than two years.

Did Elijah overstep the mark by arranging an instant cremation for 100 innocent men? It does seem a little extreme, to say the least, to torch men who after all were simply obeying orders. But we need to take a step back and think again. Ahaziah was doing far more than issuing a warrant for the arrest of Elijah. He was trying to throw a punch at God himself. He was endeavouring to maintain the awful horrors of Baal worship: child sacrifice, sexual deviancy and apostasy. How many thousands of innocents would lose their lives, either to death or degradation, if the notion that 'there was no God in Israel' became popular belief? The stakes were massively high. A few were judged in order to grab the nation's attention, so that the whole nation would not fall under God's curse.

We should also remember the attitude of the third captain, who very sensibly climbed down off his arrogant high horse and was spared as a result. If he did this, presumably the other two unfortunate captains before him could have done the same.

It was Elijah's last public act in the national life of Israel, although there was one other incident which we shall look at very briefly, when Elijah sent an international prophecy by mail.

The letter was addressed to Jehoram, the King of Judah—*not* Jehoram King of Israel. (They both reigned at the same time, adding to the confusion, and to make it worse they were related by marriage!) Jehoram of Judah had made the incredible mistake of marrying one of Ahab and Jezebel's daughters, a lovely specimen called Athaliah who inherited her mother's tendency to be overloaded with demons. When you marry the daughter of such a mother, it's likely you'll get somewhat tainted in the process. Judah's Jehoram began to follow the old and depressing road of Baalism, murder and all the rest. At this point there were actually two kings leading Judah (not an unusual situation—kings often rode 'tandem' during the hand-over period), so Jehosophat and Jehoram ruled together. This must have been the case, because Jehosophat outlived Elijah—and Elijah didn't send a letter from the grave. It was during the transitional period that the letter was written.

Jehoram had no excuse—his father Jehosophat had been a good man. Elijah's letter pronounced a curse on his people, his children, his wives and his possessions, and finally announced that he would die of a disease of the bowel.

Six years later, after a two-year illness, the unrepentant King died in agony. His is one of the saddest epitaphs in the Bible: 'His subjects did not light a bonfire in mourning for him as had been done for his ancestors . . . nobody was sorry when he died . . . they buried him in David's city, but not in the royal tombs.'

Once again Elijah's prophetic ministry had hit the target

dead centre with devastating accuracy—although he never saw the fulfilment of that particular prophetic word. In fact, he probably left the letter with Elisha, who either delivered it personally or had one of the younger 'sons of the prophets' act as postman. By the time Jehoram went down with terminal intestinal disease, Elijah was long gone.

So Elijah's public ministry drew to a close. At the beginning of this chapter I remarked that his caseload wasn't especially heavy for the long fifteen-year period between Carmel and his translation. So what else did he do with his time?

I believe that he probably laboured in the rebuilding and reviving of the prophetic colleges that began to flourish again during that period. These close-knit communities, which ate (but not necessarily lived) together were usually headed up by a chief known as the 'Father'. They were not monastic in the traditional sense—Elisha performed a miracle for 'the wife of a man from the company of the prophets' (2 Kings 4:1)—but they did live in community. So much did they flourish under Elisha's later direction that one of the schools had to build a new community to house the growing numbers.

They travelled around in processions, playing lyres, tambourines, flutes and harps, dancing and shouting their prophetic utterances. Samuel was a leader of one of these early guilds (1 Sam 19:20). They were so filled with an infectious enthusiasm for Yahweh, that occasionally even the unwitting spectator would fall under the prophetic anointing. Their effect upon the young Saul after being anointed for kingship was remarkable. Samuel declared that after meeting with a school he would be 'changed into a different person' (1 Sam 10:6), and: 'A procession of prophets met him; the Spirit of God came upon him in power' (1 Sam 10:10). Apparently the schools provided a launching pad and home base for leading itinerant prophets, gathering together for consultation and debriefing whenever the itinerants returned home from their journeys.

Jezebel almost succeeded in wiping out these guilds, but originally there must have been many schools, because the double agent Obadiah succeeded in hiding two schools away without the Queen even noticing the fact.

However, these two were the only schools that remained. In the fifteen-year period after Carmel, the schools doubled in size until there were some 200, perhaps in three schools, one of which may have settled in the Carmel area. These schools were to survive and outlive those who plotted to wipe them out—so Elijah's investment must have been well placed. It's possible that they survived for hundreds of years. There are hints of New Testament guilds in the book of Acts. Agabus, the man who only prophesied twice in the book of Acts (famine and the arrest of Paul) was probably part of a Jerusalem based guild which travelled to Antioch (Acts 11:27). Agabus was no weird lone wolf. He was a man in relationship, and he prophesied out of that secure context. Perhaps Elijah lectured his 'sons' long and hard about the perils of lonely ministry—and his teaching legacy lived on right through to the New Testament church. Thus the budding prophets became known as the 'sons of the prophets', expressing something of the family spirit that developed between them. And it's a title that Amos refers to some ninety years later: 'I was neither a prophet nor a prophet's son' (Amos 7:14).

In addition to his work with the schools, Elijah invested a great deal into his friendship with the budding successor, Elisha.

In short, Elijah became a discipler.

9

Elijah the Discipler

It happens to every preacher—particularly those who are unfortunate enough to be leading churches where most of the preaching is done by one person. You are sweating your way through a mountain of textbooks as you seek to prepare yet another talk, when a few devastatingly discouraging questions surface: 'How much of this preaching really makes any difference to people's lives?'

'Is Sunday's stirring rhetoric likely to be diluted to a vague memory on Monday, and completely forgotten by Wednesday?'

'How much can the presentation of information and truth alone really change people?'

These are uncomfortable but very important questions when you consider that many churches rely almost exclusively on a pulpit-generated programme of personal growth. Preaching is considered to be the central, vital ingredient to help bring Christian maturity. But is it enough?

The answer, from a biblical perspective, and specifically from the story of Elijah, has to be a resounding 'no!'. The command of Christ to the church is to go way beyond merely imparting information to people in the hope that 'the word will not return unto them void' (a handy little quote, mostly taken completely out of context). Young

Christians don't grow as a result of picking up truths generally scattered on Sundays from the man or woman 'at the front': rather the costly, often frustrating, but ultimately rewarding strategy for every believer's development was presented in the parting words of Christ before his ascension: 'Go and make disciples'(Mt 28:19).

This was the method that Elijah successfully used in order to shape Elisha to be his successor. This was the method that Jesus used with the Twelve. This was the strategy that he not only modelled for us, but commanded us to adopt. So why is it that most Western Christians have never been discipled by others, and their survival is more a testimony of their tenacity combined with the grace of God? Why is it that preaching is the central feature of most churches, rather than discipling? Why do some Christians seem to view the suggestion that they should make their lives accountable to others and walk in honest and open relationships as at best an invasion of their privacy, and at worst a heretical theory to be avoided like the plague?

Greek versus Hebrew: foundational comments on discipling

The church has adopted an approach to teaching which could be described as a Greek model, where liberal amounts of information are dispensed by an 'expert' in a classroom-type setting. The model is, 'I talk, you make notes and listen—and learn.' The accumulation of information is seen to be a sufficient process of education. With its plethora of Bible studies, sermon series and study notes, the church has almost fully relied upon the Greek approach—despite the fact that Jesus only used the 'mass distribution of information' approach when talking to large crowds.

With his disciples he used a completely different, Hebrew approach. In the culture of the day, disciples of a particular teacher or rabbi would commit themselves to travel with and live alongside their master. Teaching would be given in a small group environment, with plenty of time for discussion, interaction and lively debate. Following on from this, the disciple would be invited to live out what he had learned—a 'hands on/apprenticeship/ now you try it' type of approach. This was the strategy that Jesus adopted, giving greater explanations of his public discourses in private interactive sessions with the Twelve, and providing them with a workshop environment where they could develop and try out the truth—which wasn't learned until practised.

The heavy shepherding debacle

Another reason for the lack of discipleship in Western churches is the suspicion that has been aroused by the so-called 'shepherding movement' of the seventies and eighties. The worst examples of this abusive and unbiblical teaching were to be found in North America, but diluted versions floated across the Atlantic and were adopted in the UK. In this pyramid system of authority, everyone was 'covered' by another Christian, who seemed to exert massive control over the 'disciple's' life. Independent personal decision-making was viewed with suspicion, as even the minutest details of daily living were submitted for a decision from on high.

Many of the stories that circulated to discredit the shepherding movement were gross exaggerations, but it is clear that the shepherding movement fostered an atmosphere of manipulation, domination and control, and also nurtured the idea of leadership being a hierarchy with its pyramidic approach. As John Noble says, 'The only pyramids are in Egypt'—and we all know what Egypt represents: slavery, bondage and oppression.

Leaders are never told to demand submission; rather the command is given to believers to submit themselves willingly—and when this strategy is reversed, domination and control result.

However, the church typically overreacts and swings wildly like a pendulum from one end of the theological spectrum to the other, the result being that all forms of authority and accountability are still treated by some with great suspicion. In some forums the word 'discipleship' became offensive as it was loaded with oppressive connotations—and, in many cases, local church gatherings took on the style of a lecture group for numbers of gathered individuals rather than a body interrelated and interdependent. Where this pendulum swing takes place, the teaching programme tends to centre on need-related topics in an attempt to resource the individual and help him or her grow (which should be done in the context of discipling), rather than investigating meatier issues of doctrine or weighty social issues. Leadership becomes feedership, and the church becomes a carnival that celebrates individuality (and the individual joins and leaves the church if he's not being fed or his needs aren't being met) rather than a relational, integrated family who are sharing the life of God together.

We need men and women with the spirit of Elijah and Elisha. And discipling is the only way that they are going to be reproduced.

Elijah and Elisha: one plus one equals dynamite

What is the vital ingredient that separates hierarchical shepherding from biblical discipleship? The answer is just one word: friendship. Discipling is not 'people management', or 'personnel development'; it is the sharing of the life of God in the context of real, loving friendship. So it was with Elijah and Elisha: the younger man becomes a true son in the faith to the older; there are tears when they finally have to part. This is friendship, yet more than mere friendship. A kingdom relationship has been established.

Roger Forster has rightly remarked that many churches splinter because true kingdom relationships were never established; rather a group of nice people came together, tried to like each other, but when differences of opinion or conflict arrived (as in all human relationships they inevitably do), then those relationships broke down, because they were never rightly founded in the first place.

The moment we begin to look upon those whom we care for pastorally as projects, cases or counsellees, we run the risk of developing an unhelpful and certainly unbiblical mindset. Jesus sits down with a bunch of feuding disciples who frequently strolled around with their brains in neutral and their mouths in fifth gear, and calmly announces that they are far more than servants: 'I have not called you servants—I have called you friends.'

These are the kinds of relationships that Paul enjoyed, causing him to write to his good friends at Philippi with such depth and obvious affection: 'You whom I love and long for, my joy and crown' (Phil 4:1). This is no empty sentimentality. To the same people he writes: 'I have you in my heart . . . God can testify how I long for all of you with the affection of Christ Jesus' (Phil 1: 7–8).

Such is the heart of the discipler.

In Revelation Church, of which I am a part, the primary discipling unit is the house group. We have rejected the unbiblical clergy/laity divide, where the senior ministry within the local church has to be a pastor (whether or not that happens to be his or her calling from God), realising that it is impossible for one person to care for hundreds of people, even when that person is assisted by an army of staff in order to help carry the load.

The Reformers rejected the idea of this special priesthood as being utterly unbiblical 300 years ago, and then brave but pragmatic Luther started to ordain Lutheran ministers . . . and so the church still clutches to the idea.

Rather, we are wanting to see a pastoring/discipling church, where in the context of a safe small group environment individuals feel loved and cared for.

That does not mean we are fixed into a rigid structure where care can *only* take place in that context. To operate that idea would be to function in a rigid system, a management structure, rather than in relationships. To that end there are criss-crossing lines weaving all over the church as we care for one another outside of that basic model. Why? Because we are friends. And kingdom friendships are relationships with a purpose. We want to bear one another's burdens, and 'spur one another on towards good works'.

Because friendship is the key, we are free to confront one another—a vital key to growth. I have ministered in hundreds of churches in the last few years, and in so many of them there are people holding down positions of responsibility who really shouldn't be doing that task. Increasingly it becomes apparent to everyone in the church that 'Fred' is not really a worship leader. He really has a heart for it, but after ten years his singing still creates agony across the congregation and evidently God is not equipping Fred with the necessary grace required for the job. However, no one says anything, for fear that Fred will be offended or hurt. After all, he says that 'worship is *his* ministry'. So Sunday after Sunday, the public agony continues without relief. The small group of leaders don't feel able to bite the bullet on the issue. Fred will probably leave the church if they do. Better left well alone. . . .

But friends tell the truth, even when it hurts. Disciples are open to discovering their own blind spots, even when it hurts. Discipling provides the safe arena of love and commitment in order that God's people might reach their highest potential. This kind of confrontation is redemptive; an act of faithfulness among friends. Beware the person who refuses to learn. He or she is very dangerous to the body of Christ. And be careful of people who can only accept correction from those whom they perceive to be in higher authority to them. We are *all* called to submit ourselves *to one another*—not just to leaders—out of reverence for Christ.

Discipling: a costly privilege

To enjoy anything of value, there is a price to be paid. So it is with discipling. Elisha evidently came from a rich family—he was ploughing with six oxen when he received his call, which is the cultural equivalent of driving a shiny new Mercedes.

Elijah had known nothing of the protected environment that affluence can create. He lived a rough-and-ready, hand-to-mouth existence. After all, he did come from a bedouin background.

However, Elisha had a kingdom value system: he knew that to follow the call of God would result in a life far more significant and dynamic than the easy life lived by a pampered little rich kid. He turned his back on comfort and security, and began a new life of learning with the camel-skinned Elijah as his master.

To be discipled will always be costly. Mark's Gospel doesn't forget to remark that Peter and his friends 'left their nets to follow Christ'. In my church, I am privileged to be surrounded by many people who have made a choice to be disciples of Christ, whatever the cost. I think of Mary, a bright, gifted young woman with impressive architectural qualifications who could be climbing the yuppie ladder and enjoying a very comfortable lifestyle, who chooses instead to go into schools telling kids about Jesus. At one stage she was spending two afternoons a week washing dishes in a local restaurant in order to finance herself to do this great work for God. She also happens to be a fine preacher, but that is of lesser importance. What really counts is a heart that is preoccupied with pursuing hard after God, seeking first his kingdom, thrilled by the vision, sobered by the sacrifice—but following hard after God anyway. Of such is the kingdom of heaven.

Of course, the cost is not only to the Elishas of this world. The Elijahs have to pay a price as well, because discipling can be a very stressful exercise. Even the Lord Jesus felt the stress of looking after his 'house group', and asked them, 'How long shall I put up with you?'

The disciple—willing to serve

Elijah knew that a lengthy period of preparation was needed before Elisha would be ready to take over his mantle. All leadership, without exception, needs to be proved. An academic qualification or graduation from a Bible college or seminary is no proof whatever of calling to Christian leadership—all that is proved by degrees and diplomas is that information has been gathered (usually Greek style) and that this information has been retained and reported back in an examination context. Paul reminds us that elders should first be tested—and only those with a servant heart can hope to pass this biblical test.

Elisha is known as Elijah's 'attendant' (1 Kings 19:21) who would 'pour water on the hands' of his master (2 Kings 3:11). This hand-washing routine was normally only performed by women in the culture of the day, but such was the servant heart of the prophet-in-the-making that he was willing to do anything to serve and bless.

Elisha also served as a travelling companion who wouldn't go away, even when Elijah was tempted to go into his 'I want to be alone' mode. This two-by-two approach is a vital principle that all those who travel in ministry need to adopt. As I write these words, I am sitting in a hotel in snowbound Eastern Colorado, where I am speaking in a great church for four days. I've been away from my family for some ten days, and I miss them a lot. But I do have my friend Al, himself a busy church leader, who has taken nearly three weeks out of his own hectic schedule to come on this trip with me—to pray, to serve, to laugh, to encourage. The term we use for this function is 'to carry the bags'! What a difference this makes to my perspective!

There are still pressures. I am still desperate to get home to be with my wife, Kay, and Kelly and Richard. But as I travel nearly 15,000 miles in the next few days, there is someone who I know is committed to standing with me; watching my back during vulnerable moments. No wonder Jesus sent his disciples out 'two by two'. God's ideas are always the best, and we do well to follow them. And of course, Al is being served as well, in that he is having his eyes opened to a new culture, and to churches that are quite different from anything he has experienced back home. In a sense, he will never be the same again; nor will the church he leads.

The Elijah/Elisha strategy is a dynamic principle that I believe needs to be a pattern of ministry for those who travel.

The discipler: reproducing ourselves

Before Elijah was taken away from Elisha, the younger man was given an open-ended award certificate: 'What do you want me to do for you?' Elisha responded like a true son in the faith, by asking for the traditional inheritance of the first-born son: 'Give me a double portion of your spirit.' These two men had forged a solid gold friendship over the ten years they were together. They were more than colleagues; friends even. They were like father and son. So much of Elijah had rubbed off onto his assistant that now, when they were about to be parted, Elisha basically says, 'I want to be like you, Dad—only twice as powerful!'

Notice that no rebuke or correction comes from Elijah; no pseudo-humble disclaimer: 'Don't ask to be like me, son. You should emulate God alone.' No, Elijah knows that through all his successes and failures, God has been with him, anointing, shaping, developing him, and now he is a man worthy of being copied.

Like Paul, who years later wrote to his friends and said, without apology, 'Be followers of me, as I follow Christ,' so all leaders need not only to be living lives that are worthy of emulation, but should also seek to reproduce their heart and gifting in others. While we do not ever want to make clones of ourselves, we need to be spending time with others so that our trials and struggles, as well as our victories and successes, will be of service to others whom God is calling.

I am convinced that everyone, no matter how senior they are in leadership, needs a mentor. I was recently in a church where it was obvious that the main leader had a real Elijah-type anointing. He could have been a personal resource to many younger sons in leadership, but being a man of natural and genuine humility, he was struggling with the idea that he had much to give on this level. God prompted me to prophesy over him that he would be a man who would be approached by others requesting 'a double portion of his spirit', and that he was to respond to requests like this freely and gladly, recognising that it was God who was calling him to this.

Three days later, I was in another church, and felt very strongly that the young, successful leader of that congregation should be among those who should go to the previous leader and allow him to be something of a father/mentor. The second leader agreed with this. Imagine my surprise when that evening, a lady came to the platform and prophesied over the leader that God was saying that 'he could have a double portion of the spirit of Elijah'! God is certainly *for* mentoring, calling us to give authority to others to speak into our lives so that we might be shaped for significance.

Truly, Elijah the lone ranger had died on the eerie mountainside of Sinai. A team player had emerged—or perhaps the analogy of team coach is more fitting.

He was about to leave, but he had built well in Elisha his son and in the schools of prophets—his true sons in the faith. Now all that remained was a final farewell tour to say goodbye to the schools. The time was drawing near for the great man to go on to higher things.

10

Curtain and Encore

A decade of friendship had been forged between them: 3,000 days and nights of laughter, tears and training as he had shadowed the great man who was also his father and friend. How many times had he sat enthralled as he heard one more time about the blaze of Carmel? What anger had raged in his heart, clenching his fists and furrowing his brow, when he had heard the story of poor, innocent, noble Naboth! Perhaps Elisha had wept openly when he heard about the agony of Sinai, when his master had almost lost his grip on life and sanity; hope put to death, then resurrected again when God walked by.

Ten long years to get to that place where each man could almost tell the other's thoughts, anticipate the other's words, predict the other's responses. And so now Elisha must have known that something epic was taking place as they began their tour of the schools, beginning at Gilgal, then seven miles south onto Bethel, and then downhill to Jericho, the last stage of the journey. It seemed like all those with a prophetic heart knew. Elijah was going to be taken away. At each place, a prophet told Elisha, 'Your master is leaving,' and they seemed to want to make a fuss about it, but though he knew they were right, he wanted to guard the older man's emotions; to protect him from a succession of tearful, heart-rending farewells. So his response was simply: 'Hold your peace.'

We do well to remember that this tour was not just to say goodbye. The two men were in fact doing just exactly what they had been doing for the last ten years: building up the schools. Elijah was about to leave the earth, but such was the order and rhythm of his life that he continued his regular routine. No special time was needed to make peace with God and man. He lived as a man ready to die at any time. He was like John Wesley who, when asked what he would do if he knew he had just three days to live, replied: 'I should just do the work which I had already planned to do: ministering in one place; meeting my preachers in another; lodging in yet another, till the moment came that I was called to yield my spirit back to Him who gave it.'

That's the way to live!

So at last, with fifty of the sons trailing a way behind, they came to Jordan, where 555 years before Israel had celebrated the God who was bigger than Pharaoh. There were two final steps to take before God called 'time' for Elijah: a miracle and a mantle.

*   *   *

Elijah took off his cloak, rolled it up, and slapped the muddy waters of the Jordan. As the swirling waters began to boil and recede, drawn back by an invisible hand, Elisha saw completely his place in history. He recognised that the God of Moses, the God of Joshua, the God of Father Elijah, was also his God. As the waters submitted to a slap, Elisha tasted personal destiny. But as they walked through the parted waters without fear, there was one final amen to come.

'I'm about to be taken from you. What special favour can I do for you?' Elijah asked. And the younger, balding man did not hesitate to ask for a double portion of his spirit. Elijah's response seems a little strange at first glance: 'If you see me when I am taken from you, it will be yours—otherwise not.' Elijah wasn't playing games here: heads-I-win-tails-you-lose. This was no game of sleight of hand. It was imperative that Elisha see the horsemen and chariots of Israel. There would be many trials to come. Times when he would need to recall the day when God's marines touched down on earth and took a faithful man home. Times when he would need to remember that there is far more to see than most human eyes see. In 2 Kings 6, he later had to pray for his own servant, 'Give him eyes to see what I see.' I believe that Elisha's ability to see the unseen—his 20/20 vision of faith—was sparked by the way in which his master departed. School was in session for Elisha until the very last moment.

So they came, breathtaking and awesome: a whirlwind and a chariot of fire. The man who had known the elation of success and a depression that cried out for death was lifted up by the God whom he had loved. Jezebel thrown down to the dogs; the peasant from Gilead lifted up to a divine embrace. Certainly he was no angel. He made too many mistakes for that—just like the rest of us. His life was an epic story of the ordinary kissed by the Eternal; as J. Oswald Sanders put it, 'A meteor that flashed across the inky blackness of Israel's spiritual night.'

Of course there was to be a great encore. At the time of Christ, there was still an expectation that Elijah would return. Even today the Passover celebration includes a spare cup for the prophet, just in case he should choose to arrive. Some thought that John, and later Jesus, was Elijah returned. In a sense, John the Baptist picked up Elijah's ministry, calling the people back to God, preparing the way of the Lord. That's why Jesus called John 'Elijah'. This doesn't mean that John was Elijah reincarnate, for John said emphatically that he wasn't Elijah, but he carried the same mantle.

However, Elijah was to appear on the earth one more time, on the Mount of Transfiguration, where, together with Moses, he chatted with the Lord Jesus while the disciples ran around in manic circles trying to organise a building programme. Who knows what they talked about? Is it possible that, as Jesus faced the final great step of obedience, Elijah, who did wonderfully but stopped short of God's total best, encouraged his Lord to go the whole way, pay the final price, be the ultimate radical? Perhaps one day we will know. What we do know is that this ordinary man, who was 'just like us' was given an encore of honour during those Transfiguration moments. What a God we serve, who chooses to kiss the ordinary with destiny! Perhaps it's because he doesn't have anything or anybody else to choose from. As my friend Paul Gower says, 'God doesn't call heroes. He makes them.'

*   *   *

The whirlwind subsided, and the swirling sands began to thin and settle. Elisha, his heart a pounding fist, picked himself up off the soft sand where he had pushed his body down as the angels of God came.

As he stood to his feet, he knew: the shooting star that

was Elijah was gone. And the condition for him to receive the double portion had been fulfilled. He had seen Elijah go; he had seen the chariots and their riders—warriors from another world.

Time for work.

Postscript

While writing this book, I came across a poem which was written by Graeme Wylie, who has been working hard to establish a church in Galway, Southern Ireland. The path for Graeme has not been easy, but he is one of many who have stood up for God in the face of hostility. He is a modern-day Elijah.

Graeme himself writes:

A number of years ago, I was awoken in the middle of the night and stirred to get up and pray. As I was before the Lord I felt the Holy Spirit come upon me and lead me out in intercession for the West of Ireland and for the church of Jesus Christ to be established there.

We had already been working in Galway for a number of years and had felt the uphill battle to plant a church in a very beautiful but spiritually barren area. At times we had felt like giving up because it seemed impossible and the difficulties insurmountable. Yet at the same time the Lord burned into my heart the sense of His calling to persevere and see the task accomplished.

In that special time with the Lord, in a little white-washed cottage near the beautiful village of Rounstone, between 3 and 4 am 'A Prayer of Dreams Yet Unfulfilled' was written, as an expression of God's desire in my heart to stick with the task of church planting in the West of Ireland, whatever the obstacles.

More recently, as we have been led to erect a 250-seater building in Galway city to house the church that has come to birth here in the last 12 years, and to serve as a base for evangelism throughout the region. . . .

A Prayer of Dreams Yet Unfulfilled

I dream and go on dreaming for I must;
A man without a dream is dead already;
He has given up the race of life;
He has not yet reached the peak and has stopped pursuing it
And turned to amble down the hill again and leave this life unfulfilled,
A man of emptiness, settling for small things, that don't really satisfy!

> He leaves no mark in this world.
> Oh God, don't let *me* be that man!

Though I may slip and fall, help me to keep on climbing,
And though each brow reveals another and the peak is yet beyond,
May I keep on pursuing, as a man possessed, possessed by God,
Moved by vision, stirred with passion, invincible within.

> May no cliff face deflect me,
> No rock fall deter me,
> No difficulty hold me back,

There are beautiful posters available which include this poem, which can be purchased from: Graeme Wylie, 35 Grangemore, Rahoon, Galway, Ireland. Profits from the sale of posters will go to the church's building fund.

And may I never, never, never head
   down that hill again
And let life's goal elude me!

Oh my God, be my Beacon, my Companion,
My Guide and Helper, my Strength and Life.
May I climb in the footsteps of the One who climbed
   Golgotha's hill,
Who set his face like flint, with resolution of steel, who
   turned not back
But turned that hill into the greatest hill of history,
Achieving there the greatest victory this world has ever
   known.

He made His mark in this world, the greatest mark
That stands out more clearly now than ever
As increased millions put their trust in Him.

May He make His mark in me.
And go on living in this world, in me.
And go on climbing hills, in me.
Until *we* reach the peak,
And He sees His desires fulfilled, in me.

Index of Life Issues

(Note: Page numbers sometimes refer to a relevant passage that continues for several pages.)